Praise for *F.A.I.T.H.*

"*F.A.I.T.H.* is an inspirational book including raw, honest stories about women who have learned to let go and surrender to the power of faith in their lives. If you're stuck and wondering if you will ever break through, the real stories in this book can help! . . . These women have navigated the ups and downs of life and created amazing results for themselves and hold the light now for thousands of other women to do the same."

– Dina Proctor
Best-selling author of *Madly Chasing Peace*

"I have been listening to women's stories my whole life. As a facilitator and psychotherapist, it is my great joy to be a sacred witness to the power of women and our personal transformations. These stories are some of the best—well-written, heart-opening, tear-prompting, and mind-expanding. I really did make a deeper connection between my heart and mind. Is there anything more important for us as women than self-love? The path is beautifully demonstrated in this collection. Enjoy and be moved!"

– Anyaa T. McAndrew
Goddess on the Loose

"[These] amazing women look at, heal, and move past the pain and sadness of relationship issues, alcoholism, sexual abuse, and so much more! You are instantly uplifted by how [the authors] have applied what they've learned to their lives that you are inspired to bring more Love and F.A.I.T.H. into your own life. This is an excellent book to start and end your day, or pick up at any time you find yourself needing a little boost of hopefulness."

– Stacy Corrigan
Award-winn~~in author of Manifest Your Man~~

D0813631

F.A.I.T.H.

Finding Answers in the Heart™

F.A.I.T.H.

Finding Answers in the Heart™

Sheri Bagwell • Tammy Billups • Paula Flint
Julie Flippin • Betty Humphrey Fowler • Colleen Humphries
Nanette Littlestone • Ricia L. Maxie • Michelle Mechem
Linda Minnick • Laina Orlando • Bonnie Salamon
Randi Shapiro • Mindy Strich

WORDS OF PASSION • ATLANTA

F.A.I.T.H. – FINDING ANSWERS IN THE HEART

Published by Words of Passion, Atlanta, GA 30097.

Book Production: Nanette Littlestone
Editorial: Nanette Littlestone
Cover and Interior Design:
        Nanette Littlestone and Peter Hildebrandt

To receive a free e-mail newsletter delivering inspirational tips and updates about *F.A.I.T.H.*, register directly at http://www.FindingAnswersInTheHeart.com.

ISBN: 978-0-9960709-0-4

Dedicated to those
who willingly choose
to take the next step
on their spiritual journey.
May you always
have F.A.I.T.H.

Contents

Introduction

We're born, we live, we die, and if that's what you think life is all about, put down this book. Right now. You don't need faith. Not the way I did.

According to Merriam-Webster, faith is defined as: 1) belief and trust in and loyalty to God; 2) belief in the traditional doctrines of a religion; 3) firm belief in something for which there is no proof; 4) complete trust. Those definitions are fine on paper, but belief and trust are difficult to measure.

Most of my life I've struggled with the concept of faith. I grew up in a nonreligious household where there was no training, no emphasis on God, nothing that would give me faith in the unknown. I had scientific proof that the sun would rise each morning, that fall would follow summer, that I would grow older each year. But faith in God, faith in myself to achieve my dreams? Hardly.

F.A.I.T.H.

I wanted to be someone special. I wanted to do something extraordinary with my life. If I needed faith to accomplish that, great. But how did I get it?

You just have it, some people told me. Others said I would find it through prayer. For someone without a religious background, prayer seemed as uncommon and uncertain as faith. Over the years I circled the question and never found the answer.

In addition, I hid behind the shell of protection. Hard, crusty, and almost impenetrable, it served me well for many years. But as I grew older and experienced more of life, the shell began to hold me back. How could I be the brilliant and amazing woman I desired to be if I was afraid to venture out? How would people recognize my light if I failed to speak up?

There are various expressions for paying attention to that higher knowing: trust your gut; if it feels good, do it; go with the flow. Albert Einstein stated, "the intuitive mind is a sacred gift . . . I believe in intuition and inspiration; at times I feel certain I am right while not knowing the reason." It sounds easy to follow until you're in a predicament that forces a decision. While you writhe in agony, wondering what to do, which way to go, the answer is right there for you. In your heart.

Neurologist Dr. Andrew Amour from Montreal, Canada discovered that the heart's nervous system contains around 40,000 neurons that communicate with the brain. Yes, the heart and brain actually talk. And if the heart can "communicate," then it's not so farfetched to believe that it plays a large part in our daily decisions.

But many of us fail to tune in. Some people have an uncanny ability to know which path to take. Others of us seem to falter every step of the way. I could make the easy decisions about what groceries to buy or movie to see. With enough information, I could purchase a car, hire a decorator, even choose a house. But when it came to my career or my future goals, helplessness took the wheel.

My dreams are not your dreams. My questions are not your questions. But I know your pain. I know your despair. I used to be afraid. Perhaps the situations in this book will spark a memory of yours. Something the authors say will remind you of something you said or did or felt. In that, dear reader, we are one. There are universal laws and universal emotions. We all know love, hate, anger, fear. We've all felt sadness, joy, grief, happiness. We all desire to live in blissful ecstasy. But . . .

That but is the catch, the big pit that we've fallen into and can't seem to get out of. We want to be rich, have terrific careers, travel, save the planet, be in love, be happy. But something keeps us from it. Something gets in the way and turns our dreams into mush.

You *can* learn how to steer your life in the direction you choose. It's not too late to start. Your future is now. I did it, with all of my resistance. The other authors in this book did it. And if we can, then you can too.

All it takes is a little F.A.I.T.H.—Finding Answers in the Heart.

We must let go of the life we have planned, so as to accept the one that is waiting for us.

– Joseph Campbell

Julie Flippin
Dodging Bullets

We never know the exact moment when our lives will change forever. There is usually no warning, it just happens. That was my experience when I was eight years old and my parents wanted to have a "family meeting" with me and my ten-year-old sister. I had such a funny feeling in my stomach, it almost hurt with nervousness. I knew that something was wrong. We had never had a family meeting before. My legs were shaking as I joined my family at the table and wondered what they were going to talk to us about.

What was even stranger was their question. They wanted to know if we thought they should get a divorce! It was like the floor dropped out below me. A jolt ran down my arms and I simply couldn't think of one thing to say. I barely understood what "divorce" meant, but I knew it was not good. I remember there wasn't much of a conversation.

It was like sitting with people and knowing they were all talking, but I couldn't grasp what they were saying. Tension filled the air when someone suggested that it would be a good idea to get a divorce. I heard that loud and clear and felt so confused. What impacted me more was the scared look on my mother's face. If Mom was scared, then I was scared, and I watched her more than listened. Something was building and my throat was tightening and my stomach started aching. Suddenly Dad jumped up from the table, crashed his chair to the floor behind him, and ran into the bedroom. I had never seen him so angry. He had a wild look in his eyes and he was snarling. He seemed eight feet tall and four feet wide.

He ran back out and pointed his shotgun at us and screamed that he was going to kill us if we didn't get out. There was a metallic taste in my mouth and my limbs just froze. It felt like someone punched me in the stomach and I couldn't breathe. All the air emptied from the room and there was an eerie silence that seemed to crackle accompanied by the sweet, sickening smell of fear. Everything seemed to move in slow motion.

I didn't know what to do. I think my mother knew instinctively not to move as she realized we were in a life or death situation. All I remember after that was slowly backing out of the room, out of the house, whispering, "Okay, Dad. Okay, Dad."

When I left the house I did not scream, nor did I run for help. I ran and hid in our tent trailer beside the house and stayed there. For a long time.

I wish I could tell you that was the last time I walked away from something I feared.

I don't know how or when I left the trailer. I know no one died that day, not physically, although it felt like a part of me died. No one came to get me or checked on me. At some point I just came out and acted as if nothing happened. I became an expert at that and keeping my feelings of fear, anxiety, and inferiority safely tucked away inside so no one would know, so I could "be" on the outside whatever I thought was "expected" of me.

My father's behavior continued over the next nine years. I never knew what I was going to come home to—my mother's clothes being burned in the fireplace, the shotgun and shells left on the table with a note saying "when you go to sleep tonight I'm going to use this on you," a suicide attempt by my Dad. Nine years of absolute and utter insanity.

We reached out to the police on two separate occasions because we were so afraid for our lives. We didn't dare call them before my dad passed out. When they finally arrived, they made two things really clear. They didn't feel sorry for us, and it was "our" problem. When we showed them the shotgun, the note, the bullets, they just told us to be careful and they hid the gun behind the curtains in the living room. When I realized they were not going to do anything else I was terrified. Devastated. I hated them for that. This added to the depth of my unimportance on such a deep level. We were truly on our own and no one was going to rescue us.

I never told my friends, teachers, or neighbors what went on in our house. The "secret" hosted a lot of shame and embarrassment. It was as though what my dad did was because there was something wrong with *me*. I didn't know he was ill. I thought if only I was prettier or smarter or I didn't make mistakes then Dad wouldn't want to kill me. I felt very unlovable. Nothing I did was enough. And I promised myself I would never be like him.

Over those years I learned how to survive. I learned not to trust myself because every time I thought someone was my friend, I would be betrayed. My worst fears became my reality. When I was in grade 9, my family decided to move to another city. I was afraid to leave my hometown but Mary had just moved from the city we were moving to. We talked a lot about me moving to her city and she promised to let her friends know I was coming. She would "pave the way" for me. I was so relieved. About a month after my family moved, one of Mary's friends told me that Mary hated me and no one in this new city wanted to be my friend. The shock felt the same as the day my father walked out of that room with a shotgun.

I thought things had changed for the better with my first boyfriend. Oh my goodness, I don't think anything felt as wonderful as someone picking me and liking me. Until my "best friend" decided she liked him (of course she was gorgeous and popular) and he dropped me immediately and started dating her. I covered my hurt by telling her it was no problem, that it didn't bother me.

So I learned not to trust myself. I also decided not to trust people 100%, to always hold back, because somehow that would prevent me from being hurt. People could change and turn at any given moment so I had to be on guard. When they did turn on me, my brain literally froze and I often was unable to move. Then I wondered how I would act when my body finally was able to move. Would everyone think I was crazy? There was so much shame attached to this. But I was a survivor and I learned how to cope and manage, so I packed up my life skills and went out into the world to try and find love.

I wanted to be loved so badly. Somehow I felt if I was loved, I would be okay, I would be worth it, and *then* I could trust, *then* I would be whole, *then* I would have a life.

Thirty-three years later, I woke one morning having come off a five-day binge knowing that I could no longer live the way I had been living. I had been partying for five days straight and felt sick and disgusting and hopeless. The pain of trying to be good enough, pretty enough, smart enough, and lovable had become so great that I turned to alcohol for relief. As a child, I didn't know that my dad was a raging alcoholic. I was an adult before I was able to put a name to it. I had promised myself I would never be like my dad and

I wasn't, on the outside. I didn't threaten to kill anyone or myself. I didn't terrorize people. But I was like my dad in so many other ways. I turned to alcohol to relieve the pain within. I was emotionally unavailable, I bullied people to get my own way, I felt powerless so I overpowered people emotionally to feel safe and secure, and I didn't know how to give or receive love fully. The shame, guilt, and embarrassment of feeling so unlovable were so great that I had become just like my dad. And it just about killed me.

That morning I thought if this is it, if this is all there is, I don't know if I can continue on any longer. Hopelessness and despair had become my constant companions. But something happened to me that day. It was as if my soul finally cried out in desperation for relief. Dear God, *please* help me!

There wasn't a flash of light or a heavenly being that appeared. That would have made believing so much easier. It wasn't that I didn't believe in God, I just didn't think God believed in me. But something inside me shifted that morning. I wasn't ready to give up. I had two amazing children who didn't deserve what I was giving them. If I couldn't do it for myself I would do it for them. So I got up, got dressed, went to work, and started looking for help with my drinking. I knew if only I quit drinking everything would be okay. And I did, I found help. A wonderful 12-step program that literally saved my life. People accepted me for who I was without judgment and I began my road of recovery.

Every time I did something else to "heal" I would think, there, that's it, I've done it. *Now* I will live happily ever after. I didn't know for a long time that this life is a journey. There is no destination, no "happily ever after." Not in the fairy tale sense, not for me. I believe we are here to expand and know joy in new and endless ways. The path to joy, for me, has been by experiencing contrast in my life—realizing what I didn't want so I would have a clearer understanding of what I did want.

I have been working through the layers of old limiting beliefs that kept me stuck and living in limitation instead of possibility. I have been willing to have the breakdowns which lead to amazing breakthroughs that brought me incredible joy with possibilities to live broader, and the gift to receive and give love in ways that had escaped me.

Six years later, I decided to start my own accounting and bookkeeping business and operated that business for about five years. Although I enjoyed my business, I had such a yearning in my heart to help other people who understood feelings of hopelessness. I knew that my journey and the work I had done—the 12-step program, the counseling, the hundreds of books I had read, and the energy work—had brought me to a place of grace in my life with so many blessings that I wanted to give back. I wanted to help people. I had absolutely no idea how I could do that, but I could not ignore the deep calling I felt. So I meditated on it. I didn't know what the next steps would be. I felt blind and deaf so I kept my prayers simple. "Tell me in a way I can understand. Show me in a way so I will know." I was never really sure exactly who I was praying to, but over the years I became peaceful about not really having to "know," but believing that I was connected and part of something that was magnificent.

One morning I had a wonderful meditation—20 minutes passed and it felt like I had just closed my eyes. I came out of it with a feeling of such joy and a strong knowing that I would be shown how I could give back. (It would have to be clear for me, because I have to be hit over the head about five times before I get most things. Learning to trust my feelings and intuition—my heart messages—have been my greatest teachings.)

Later that day a client came over and he was talking about a weekend program he had signed up for to learn a healing modality. It was designed to help people identify and change the limiting beliefs that had kept them stuck which prevented them from living the life they truly wanted.

As I listened to him I felt a tingling that started in my toes and worked its way up and out the top of my head. It was delicious! I felt like I had been hit over the head in the nicest way possible!

I felt so inspired I immediately called Lisa (who was giving the Core Belief Engineering workshop) to inquire about any openings. Of course there was a spot open. Two weeks later I was at the workshop my client spoke of. I was surprised when I was chosen to go through a five-hour process with the teacher to model the work she was teaching. I had a major breakthrough that day which was awesome. I felt very inspired to learn this technique. But by the end of the second day something had shifted. I was overwhelmed. I felt completely incapable of learning this work and wondered even if I did, who would ever want to work with me. My old feelings of unworthiness surfaced and I shut down due to fear of the unknown. I left word that I would not be completing the workshop.

I couldn't think of one other thing in the weeks to come. My mind constantly badgered me. There was another program that they offered but it cost about $20,000. I didn't have that in my bank account. But I woke up thinking about it and went to sleep dreaming about it. I was having a hard time even working because I couldn't get it out of my head. I felt excited and stirred up, so I finally surrendered to it and called Elly, the creator of the program. Since her school was on the other side of the country I knew I would have to fly back and forth for months and it would take me about a year to get certified. I signed up anyway. I carried my laptop back and forth, running my business from the plane, bed and breakfast, and my office.

The B&B where I stayed when I was at school each month was about a block from the ocean. My first morning, I went for a walk down to the ocean, and it was beautiful. The pier jutted out in the water and was surrounded by mountains. I decided to go for a walk that first morning to soothe my nerves and as I neared the pier, my heart rate increased and a storm of emotion rose up in me. This was it, this was real. It was no longer a dream. Could I actually do what I had just invested in? Could I "be enough" to make a difference in other people's lives, even my own?

By the time I reached the pier there were tears streaming down my face. I could feel the tremendous energy of the ocean and the mountains surround me and I threw my arms out to the universe and knew, knew deep within for the first time in my life I was enough. They were tears of absolute and utter joy. In the depths of my being I knew I was on purpose, doing exactly what I was meant to be doing. The part of me that was left in the tent trailer that day so many years before seemed to join my soul, and I felt whole and part of something so much greater than myself. I realized for the first time in my life I felt *love*, what real love is, complete, whole, healthy, and perfect just the way I was.

I learned to trust something I couldn't see, feel, or touch. I learned to trust myself and to accept and love who I am, warts and all, and know that I am enough. This allowed me to love and accept others in the same way. I finally realized the "betrayals" I felt didn't define who I was; they only defined the other person. So I worked on not taking things so personally. What freedom! I learned to stop blaming my father for my life and chose to take responsibility for myself and the life I had created and the life I wanted to create. But the most important thing I learned was forgiveness. Forgiveness for my father and forgiveness for myself.

The night the police refused to rescue my family I learned a crucial lesson: I was the only one who could rescue me. No one can do it for me. Someone else can hold a 100-watt light bulb for me to see the path, but I have to take those steps myself.

I feel like I've been dodging bullets my whole life, starting with my dad's gun. The bullets were my fears—fears of the unknown. It is so nice to know that I don't have to run away or dodge bullets any longer.

Taking new risks and up leveling myself and my business still feel scary and overwhelming to me at times. When they do, I just get quiet and ask to be shown in a way that I understand what I am too afraid to see or do and where the light is along the path. And then I ask for the courage to keep moving forward.

My deepest desire for you is to never ever give up, keep moving forward, and take action in your life. There is such love and joy in our growth and expansion. And if you feel like you are in a dark place along the path, just close your eyes and ask for help. I promise you this; help is always there for us.

F.A.I.T.H.

Julie Flippin, owner of Small Business Savvy, is a business coach who works with passionate small business owners who are committed to being more profitable. She takes the fear out of marketing and sales and creates strong, workable strategies for business entrepreneurs to achieve their goals.
www.smallbusinesssavvy.com

Grief can be the garden of compassion. If you keep your heart open through everything, your pain can become your greatest ally in your life's search for love and wisdom.

– Rumi

Good Grief

Could the worst day of my life turn out to be the best day too? It turns out that the day I lost my faith was also the day I discovered it. It just took me a decade or two to connect the dots.

Jerry Garcia was right when he said, "Once in a while you get shown the light in the strangest of places if you look at it right."

A few days before my 25th birthday my mother was scheduled for a surgical procedure to treat a severe case of diverticulitis. She was in enormous pain, and when nothing else seemed to work, surgery was recommended.

The day after her surgery I walked into her hospital room and overheard a conversation she was having with my grandmother, her mother, who had passed away when I was four years old.

"I'm coming, Mom," she said. "I'll be there soon." I was stunned.

In those days talking to deceased relatives landed you in the psych ward, not with your own reality television show. The doctors assured me she'd be back to herself in few days. It wasn't uncommon for post-op patients to "hallucinate" from the pain meds. Okay, I thought, doctors know best. I tried to relax and stop worrying.

An hour or so later, my cousin called from Atlanta to say she was coming to visit her next week. "You'll need to come sooner," Mom whispered. "I won't be here next week."

So much for relaxing.

I have no idea what my mother was seeing and feeling but it was definitely not from the drugs. She knew something the rest of us didn't.

My cousin was on the next flight to New York and we were back at the hospital first thing the following morning. When we arrived my mother was still out of it, agitated, confused, and somewhat incoherent. I bent down to kiss her and in a moment of lucidity she grabbed my hand and said, "I want you to go home. Go out and celebrate your birthday. Have fun." I was astonished. She barely knew where she was let alone what day it was. How could she possibly have known it was my birthday?

Every fiber in my body wanted to stay but she pleaded with me to go. So I kissed her goodbye, told her to get some rest, and assured her I'd be back soon. But the instant I walked out of her room I had a sick feeling that I would never see her again.

Culturally, I grew up Jewish but my religious upbringing was not very significant. My early childhood memories are more about death than divinity. Any faith my parents may have intended to pass down vanished after my youngest brother died of a rare infection when he was six weeks old. The year before that the only grandmother I ever knew died suddenly of a heart attack. I was four. She was fifty-six.

My mother never fully recovered from her grief. The loss of her mother, her son, and the terror of losing me overwhelmed her. It exhausted her body and consumed her mind. She was diagnosed with breast cancer, then a few years later with emphysema. Fear engulfed her while I spent most of my life fighting to break free of those same fears that were unconsciously instilled in me.

My mother passed away that night. September 29th, 1984. My 25th birthday.

I was lost. It felt as if I was walking through life in a fog. Everything seemed so surreal. When I got up the next morning she wouldn't be sitting at the breakfast table asking me what I wanted for dinner? She wouldn't be there to walk me down the aisle or see my brother graduate from college? Experience the joy of grandchildren? I couldn't wrap my brain around it. Mother's *do not die* on their daughters' birthdays!

Well, yes, sadly they do. When the people I loved left me it shook me to the core.

No one escapes life without facing pain. Pain is a catalyst that can make you or break you. Devastate or empower you. Pain will break you down and pain will break you open. Just ask any woman in labor. Like it or not, to create a new life, pain is part of the process. In the midst of it all I had the choice. Would the pain destroy or enlighten me?

My mother was a fighter, but when she decided to stop fighting she was liberated from her pain. She finally let go of her fear and her grief and in doing so she planted the seeds to one of my greatest life lessons: Courage was not the action of fighting for my life; courage was my willingness to let go. The freedom I sought was waiting on the other side of surrender.

On the first anniversary of my mother's passing I quit my job, packed my bags, and left the only home I ever knew. All my joyful childhood memories were living in the shadows of the deafening emptiness I felt every night when I went home. It was time for me to let go, to start a new chapter in my life.

So I headed south, to the place that exemplified my happiest childhood memories . . . Atlanta. Until I found a place of my own I was invited to live with my cousin. I could feel my mother smiling. She always wanted to move to Atlanta, and even more than that, she knew I always did too. Living the dream, Mom!

GOOD GRIEF

There's an old Zen story about a farmer who had worked his crops for many years. One day his horse ran away. Upon hearing the news, his neighbors came to visit. "Such bad luck," they said sympathetically.

"Maybe," the farmer replied.

The next morning the horse returned, bringing with it three other wild horses. "How wonderful," the neighbors exclaimed.

"Maybe," replied the old man.

The following day, his son tried to ride one of the untamed horses, was thrown, and broke his leg. The neighbors again came to offer their sympathy on his misfortune.

"Maybe," answered the farmer.

The day after, military officials came to the village to draft young men into the army. Seeing that the son's leg was broken, they passed him by. The neighbors congratulated the farmer on how well things had turned out.

"Maybe," said the farmer.

Maybe the worst thing that ever happens to us can also turn out to be the best.

Today my birthday is no longer a day to mourn my mother's passing. Instead, it has once again become a day of joy, celebration, and gratitude. It is a day that I remember and honor the profound and cherished connection my mother and I share. Now, then, and always.

F.A.I.T.H.

One of my favorite books, *Tuesdays with Morrie*, says it well:

> As long as we can love each other and remember the feeling of love we had, we can die without ever really going away. All the love you created is still there. All the memories are still there. You live on in the hearts of everyone you have touched and nurtured while you were here. Death ends a life, but it doesn't end a relationship. – Morrie Schwartz

And what a relationship it's been.

Not long after my mother's death I had a dream that there was a phone booth with a direct line to heaven. For ten cents you could make a call. Not many people were aware of this miracle but in my dream I was chosen to receive this information so I could "connect" and tell others. I have to wonder if this was a premonition to my becoming an energy healer. In my work today I am so grateful that I have the opportunity to help others make connections that lead to deep and profound healing.

Soon after my dream I started to find dimes everywhere. Other people tend to find pennies, I find dimes. Especially in laundry rooms. My mother was obsessed with doing the laundry. "Good morning, Mindy. Before you leave for school please throw in a load of laundry." "How was school today? Before you start your homework please fold the laundry." "Dinner's ready kids, but before we eat you need to put the clothes in the dryer!" For me, finding dimes in the laundry, well you can't make this stuff up.

My mother's passing is the singular event that continues to guide and teach me about life's deepest truths. Her presence is always around me. I hope that I've lived my life in a way that would have made her proud. "Mom, if it'll make you happy . . . I'll even do the laundry."

Mindy Strich is a certified I.E.M. Energetic Healer and owner of Healing Hearts, LLC. Locating energetic imbalances, Mindy assists clients that are experiencing physical or emotional pain to activate their bodies' natural ability to heal.
www.healingheartenergy.com

Being deeply loved by someone gives you strength, while loving someone deeply gives you courage.

– Lao Tzu

Paula Flint
Deep Freeze

The ice cold snow was a foot deep as it melted against my naked body. My heart screamed to feel something, anything! I had cried so many tears that the cells in my body completely separated themselves from my emotions. How did I get to the point where I wondered if life was worth living?

My husband and I were originally introduced at a mutual friend's house. I can't call it a date because we were simply tricked into the meeting. We were both asked to come to lunch without the other's knowledge. A couple days later, he called and asked me to go skiing. On our first date, we talked about how much we both wanted to have children. Two boys and a girl in that order and close together. We fell instantly, madly in love!

He would come to my house after he got off work and we would sit on the couch with our arms around each other and gently kiss while holding our lips together, slowly breathing in and breathing out. No talking, no moving, just touching and breathing and loving each synchronous beat of our hearts. I often wonder where did we go during those hours? Mentally? Emotionally? Spiritually? We would not stop until the TV went off the air at 2 a.m. This was in February, 1978. I was 25. He was 23.

In April we married. We had our first son ten months later and bought a home. We had our second son 15 months later. We had our daughter 15 months after that. We met, married, had three children, and bought a home in two and a half years.

From the very beginning, I did not realize that not everyone can simply choose to quit drinking. My husband continued his regular routine, while having three babies forced me to curtail my consumption. My love for our children overshadowed my need to escape into another state of consciousness. But I did not realize what a large part it would play in the drama soon to unfold.

There were subtle signs from the onset of our relationship. We picked out my engagement ring on Valentine's Day. Afterwards, we stopped by his friend's house to return a video tape. When we got back in the car he said, "I would have introduced you but I couldn't remember your name." Wow! Too much too fast! We have laughed about that many times over the years, but what was it really saying? I fell in love with an illusion constructed in my heart? Perhaps I needed years of experience to carve away the illusions that I had spent a lifetime building around my heart, my mind, and my body. But how could I know that when I was so young, innocent, forever-hopeful, and in love?

Unlike a flambé, alcohol suffocated the flame of love that had been ignited on my couch. As the intensity of life increased, so did my husband's consumption of alcohol. This altered state of consciousness intensified his need for affection while simultaneously intensifying my need to shut out the pain, disappointment, and disillusionment. I remember saying, "If you'll stop drinking and give me some emotional space, I promise I'll be there for you." How could I know that he was not hearing what I was so desperately saying?

In the mid-90s, I started a holistic healing business. About a year after opening the doors, and after much spiritual contemplation, I decided it was time to close. I was having trouble making enough money to justify staying open. At 9:00 a.m. I told the building's owner that I would be closing my doors. At 9:05 a.m. I received a call from my husband telling me that his mother had just had a debilitating stroke. She could not walk or talk and could barely feed herself. I found the two events too coincidental to ignore, so I offered to have her move in with us.

To make life even more intense, we had three teenagers all in high school and all driving. The fact that our children were 16, 17, and 18 made the experience more hectic yet, ironically, more enjoyable. They were very independent, busy young people weaving their way through life. Their grandmother had always been a part of their lives, so to have her live with us gave them the opportunity to participate in an important part of her life. It also allowed them to see that families take care of each other. Doing the right thing does not always mean doing the easy thing.

I had no idea how this decision would broaden the divide between my heart, my mind, and my body. I stuck tenaciously by my husband's side. In fact, he practically had to use a crowbar to loosen my grip. I refused to give up on him because of the deep feelings of love we shared. However, I was suffocating and desperately needed oxygen! So I did a spiritual exercise. For 21 days, I wrote the following sentence 21 times. "I am a perfect example of unconditional divine love." What I got was the opportunity to put my desire into action.

Little did I realize that things would have to get worse before they could get better. I went to see a counselor and, bless her heart, she made it worse by saying the exact wrong words during our first session. Her lack of emotional connection quite literally cut me like a knife. As an assignment, she asked me to write down what I was thinking about every time I cried. The next week, I said, "I did the assignment and it was your words that made me cry. I don't know if you did that on purpose, but I can tell you that it hurt me more than my husband already has. So here is your money for today's session. I won't be back. Please be careful with what you say to other women who are in my situation." All this did was add another check mark on the list of situations from which I needed to learn nonjudgment. It was about a week later that I found myself freezing in hell.

I wish I could say that I had an epiphany, a voice thundering in my head! "Paula, your emotions are buried so deep that you've lost touch with the gift of love!" Any deep revelation that could have helped. But, alas, there was nothing. Experience is like a faucet that relentlessly drip drip drips. With enough time the tub spills over.

It took me three years and three attempts to break the chains that bound my heart to his. The first time, I changed the locks on all the doors after he left for work. He came home to find his clothes outside neatly packed in boxes. I refused to let him in. That lasted about two days. The second time, I moved out and that lasted about two weeks. The third time, I moved out, got a divorce, and moved across the country. Even after I moved, he called to let me know how my parents were doing—they were living on their own and in their eighties. He mowed their lawn and ate dinner with them weekly. He would also call to make sure I was doing okay living all alone halfway across the country.

It was about a week after he received my letter telling him that we had to stop talking every day. He had his life in West Virginia and I had mine on the Cherokee Reservation in Oklahoma. He replied, "I got your letter. I read it, put it

in the drawer, and won't read it again, 'cause you'll be back."
One week later, I woke up with the unavoidable inner nudge
that it was time to go home. I called him and he came to get
me the next week.

Sometimes my intense desire to surrender to God's will
influences the way I perceive what's best for me. Is that
bad? Is that wrong? I don't think so. It has served me well
by allowing me to quite innocently walk into situations that
would ultimately bring pain. Only time and experience
manifest the gifts hidden deep within the folds.

I can see today that I needed to have blinders on, to
be mesmerized by our initial sensations of love. It was
necessary so that I would never lose touch with the intensity
of our beyond-the-physical-world heart connection. Upon
hindsight, would I change it? Absolutely not! The pain
allowed me to defrost some of the ice I had so skillfully built
around my heart.

I made a decision long ago that after I pass from this
world and do my past-life review I would never say, "If only
I had listened to that still small voice within, I would have
known that there was a priceless gem buried deep beneath
that snow!" I accept the wisdom I have gleaned. Every
teardrop, or lack thereof, has been well worth it.

Four years after divorcing, we remarried and are bliss-
fully happy! We had slowly chiseled away each other's
illusions so our true selves could take center stage. He no
longer drinks and I no longer have ice clogging my veins.

Paula Flint is a member of the ECK Clergy and a Life Coach with a Masters in Counseling Psychology. She draws upon 60 years of research strengthened by personal experiences to assist clients in healing their mental, emotional, and spiritual bodies. www.Lifecoach147.com

Faith is a knowledge within the heart, beyond the reach of proof.

– Kahlil Gibran

Bonnie Salamon
Powerless to Purposeful

Imagine that as a young bride, your mailbox hangs just outside your apartment door. You need only take a single step out to get the mail. Your other alternative is to reach around the corner of the door and easily grab your day's envelopes. But it takes you hours to work up the courage to do even that.

Or imagine that you have half of your grocery list items in your basket, and you absolutely *must* leave the cart where it is without checking out or having those groceries bagged. When panic strikes, the fight or flight response is so strong, there may be no understanding the actions that ensue.

And driving feels like it would be fatal as you hug the right lane and refuse to drive expressways. The thought of boarding an airplane would require months of mental preparation, and on the day of the flight, you cannot be coaxed on the plane no matter what.

These simple tasks of everyday life caused fear so over-whelming that my heart would pound, and sweat-producing, knee-buckling panic attacks would render me unable to conduct my daily desires. There are no words to adequately describe the continuous sense of doom, or the total embar-rassment and isolation that grew out of these experiences that began when I was a preteen.

Some of these episodes might last from 3 to 18 months. During the worst of these times, when I struggled to go to school, or even to be with friends, my mother used to say, "Where's your faith?" I just did not seem to be able to reach my G-d, and I thought I would suffer like this always. I had to ask *why*? I had been a person of faith, of belief that prayers were answered. I was a dutiful daughter, student, Jewess.

Such was my life as a young woman with depression and agoraphobia. This crippling chemical imbalance began when I was 12 and did not receive proper diagnosis until I was 34 . . . 22 years of not knowing when "it" would take over my life again. In those years, discussing such maladies was a "no-no" for fear that you would be ostracized, shunned, or even worse—locked away in a mental ward. Not only was it painful and debilitating, it was surreal and a life of seclusion and total loss of self.

Still, in spite of my doubts, I always knew that there was a better life waiting for me. Somehow, I would prevail. I did not know how, or when, but I hungered for that meaningful life, and crawled, walked, and then ran for the life I knew I could have.

Little by little, I pulled myself out of the abyss. After one nine-month bout with my demons, I fell in love with, and married, my true companion. Then after learning of my mother's cancer, I spiraled down, once again, for 18 months, never leaving home unless accompanied by my husband. Our only child was born in one of my "good" times. Yet, still I struggled to keep "it" (the depression and agoraphobia that didn't have names then) away from me.

Even after a correct diagnosis and medication to enable me to conquer what was necessary to have a "normal" life, the marks of those 22 years were still with me. I faced the world unsure, lacking in confidence and with doubt in my abilities personally and professionally.

I add to the list the loss of three unborn children, the death of my father and my mother, a pre-malignant condition that took my uterus, and career disappointments with one boss who sexually harassed me and another who was a Nazi sympathizer and made my work life a living hell. Yet each one of my crises did not mean the end of me, or what I came here to do, though I wasn't sure exactly what that was. While I still saw myself as a "behind the scenes" person, always supporting others, I began to gain a sense of self with each small step I took.

My "sense of self" developed as I tackled one small hurdle after another. I took a job as the Credit Manager of the Peachtree Plaza Hotel, then the world's tallest and first totally computerized hotel. Panic attacks be darned, I walked down into the dark underbelly of the hotel every day to the boss who harassed me with Nazi gestures (in a time when that was not considered harassment). I then joined a professional group and eventually became its treasurer. Wrestling with anxiety for a day before simply having to read a treasurer's report, I stood shaking to do what my office required.

When I became an entrepreneur at the age of 32, I flailed and faltered. But again, not giving in, not giving up. I knew nothing about being an entrepreneur or how to run a financial business in an industry dominated by men. Along the way, I made mistakes—hiring mistakes, taking on the wrong clients, the wrong business partner, and it was all a learning curve.

An inner knowing kept telling me that my experiences had been something I could draw on to not only help myself, but to help others as well. It wasn't only the business experiences that gave me the compassion to have a loving, peaceful work environment in my company, and to finally bring my voice into my communities. It was the miscarriages, the loss of loved ones, and other challenges that I hoped would stand for something important that I wanted to share with others so they, too, might find their inner strength.

It would be 20+ years later, in my mid-50s, that I embarked on a spiritual journey that was to totally change my direction, my connection to Spirit, and enable me to see all the joy and beauty that was readily available to me every step of my way.

Through a chance encounter, I began to delve into the spiritual and natural worlds by way of teachings from Nicole Christine (the Priest/ess Process) and Lisa Michaels (Natural Rhythms). Never again would I feel alone on the path to my answers, my truths, and my Life Purpose. Never again would I have to be alone in my struggles as I found the community of like-minded women (and men) who would be my support. Through breast cancer and some difficult times during the recent market crash, my faith, my knowing that Spirit was guiding me, and with the help of my spiritual community, I prevailed.

I truly stepped off the precipice some eight years ago when I began to study facilitation of both the Priest/ess Process and Natural Rhythms (of which I am a Charter facilitator). Taking on one of the biggest challenges of my life, I trusted, and had faith, that I could deliver programs from one hour to full days without the need to run in fear. I began to believe that I had something of value to share with my community. That I could hold a space for those struggling with their own inner demons, and help them recognize *their* inner wisdom.

I added to that a certification in Gerontology so that I might understand what is needed for a fulfilling later life. Today, my continuing search for all that Spirit has in store for me has led me to the study of Celebrancy. I am now a Certified Life Cycle Celebrant ™, performing rites for those who honor turning points on life's journeys. Our significant events deserve proper recognition. No more ignoring what has had meaning for us, but what we have hidden or not honored. Once again I have faith that Spirit has brought me to this place, and that I will be supported in celebrating, or honoring, other people's joys, sorrows, and pivotal life experiences.

The "background" person I was became the thought leader I was meant to be. Oh yes, and I now drive constantly, even making long trips alone, by car; I fly to many different parts of the world, shop with ease, and relax into sharing my own truths in individual coaching and small group circles; and I have hosted over 125 attendees for a multi-day event two years in a row.

There is no doubt that my place in the world is Spirit driven. My life has been, and continues to be, Spirit-ed and Spirit led. Understanding that my Higher Power had more in store for me than I could have ever imagined, I am grateful for my own faith, for my knowing that I must keep trying, step by tiny step, to share my truths and visions with the world. So when I hear my mother's voice ask, "Where's your faith?" I simply say it is my companion every day, hour, and minute of my life.

Bonnie Salamon's joy is to assist heart-centered, Spirit-ed individuals to live their Purpose and create the longed-for life that is theirs for the asking. She does this through one-on-one coaching, group processes, teleseminars, and celebrating life passage events through personally designed ceremonies. Her company, Autumn's Fire, is dedicated to Reigniting Passion and Purpose. www.autumnsfire.org

Only when we are no longer afraid do we begin to live.

– Dorothy Thompson

COLLEEN HUMPHRIES

Money Burnout Blues

Fear, doubt, worry, and desperation. Those can lead to a whole lot of lack. And that's where I was for over a year.

When I first started my journey into Life Coaching and speaking I was in my mid-to-late 40s. I was on top of the world. Entrepreneurship was a whole new and exciting direction for me. Initially I had no clue what to do, I just knew I was on my way to being a successful entrepreneur and I loved it.

For the first year and a half I was unstoppable. I was a manifesting machine. It was amazing! I manifested great opportunities like going to the National Publicity Summit in New York to meet the media to give them story ideas. I received my certification as a Law of Attraction Life Coach and chose to work with nurses in burnout, since I was a former burned out nurse. I even had the awesome opportunity of mentoring under Jack Canfield for a year. I looked forward to each day and all of the exciting possibilities that were there for me to explore.

And then . . . slowly . . . it all started to fall apart. I felt like I did not have any encouragement or support from my family or my boyfriend. I felt like no one was interested in what I was doing in my new career. A few friends came out for some of my presentations, but that was it. I spoke one to two times a month with two of my friends from my life coaching class. But there was no one in my immediate surroundings for me to talk to about conscious manifesting, universal energies and laws, and deliberate creation. When I did talk to different friends the main topics were always their hard lives and the bad economy.

During family gatherings, no one discussed my life coaching and speaking. If I mentioned them, they were ignored. I could see what looked like anger on my father's face. I wanted to yell, "Did anyone just hear what I said? Can anyone say, 'Good for you, Colleen? I/we are proud of you for pursuing your dreams.'" I smiled on the outside but inside I was screaming. Time after time, I sat there without any support.

With my boyfriend, it was a cycle of on and off support. After a brief breakup due to a total lack of interest in anything I was doing, he attempted to be more responsive to me about my work. But that was short-lived. I was going crazy in my mind. I silently hollered, "Why can't you be happy for me?

Why can't we talk about what's going on with my business or my seminars? Why can't you ask me how I am?"

I constantly focused on the lack of interest and support from the people closest to me.

I decided I needed to learn more information so I could be more than what and who I was. I went from seminar to seminar, from training to training. If I could show them all of the good that I was doing, my family, friends, and boyfriend would have to acknowledge me and my hard work.

Along the way I spent a lot of money. I thought I was in an abundant mindset. If I spent money towards my business, I would surely get it back. I told myself I was taking the steps in faith. Because I specialized in the Law of Attraction, I had faith the Universe would support me in my endeavors and draw to me means of financial compensation.

I did a lot of activities—networking, writing newsletters and articles, making videos, social media. Nothing happened. Where were the nurses in burnout? Didn't anyone want to get out of burnout? Mine almost cost me my job on more than one occasion. Didn't anyone want help?

It seemed like even the Universe didn't support me in my efforts.

Fear, doubt, and worry took over my mind. I knew I did not want those negative thoughts and emotions in my head and vibrating through and out of my body, but there they were.

I had a routine of self-care that consisted of meditation, journaling, chi gong, EFT (Emotional Freedom Technique/Tapping), yoga, and regular exercise. I chose two to three things to do to get myself focused and ready to start my day. But they failed to help. I became a human "doing" instead of a human "being." I was so far into my head and miles away from my heart.

One day my father stated, "I am disappointed in you. I do not believe in what you are doing and I don't like it." My boyfriend and I became more distant. I let their disinterest and disbelief affect me. My mind became filled with impoverished thoughts.

I went from "the Universe is always abundant" to "Why am I having a difficult time finding clients?" "Why can't I find any clients?" "OMG, I'm not making any money. How am I going to pay my bills?" And I spiraled down and down like Alice in Wonderland going down the Rabbit hole.

I told myself that my focus was in the wrong place. I knew I needed to pay attention to what I wanted rather than what I did not want. I knew that only I needed to believe in myself and if I focused my thoughts correctly, the Universe would deliver. *I knew it.*

But even with the meditation and other modalities, I was still stuck in all of the negative, fearful, doubting thoughts and I vibrated all of that out into the Universe. Because I doubted my abilities as a coach and speaker, I fell headfirst into the lack mindset that surrounded me.

My head was talking and I was listening. I had the heart-pounding-in-my-chest, gut-wrenching, sick-to-my-stomach-in-the-middle-of-the-night fear, where I dreaded getting up in the morning because I truly did not know what to do. Who was that person? I did not recognize her any more.

Because I felt the need to prove what I knew worked, I was in more resistance and I proved the opposite. I figured that I had to work really hard to "make it," because that was what everyone else around me talked about and believed.

And then . . . the manifesting of situations that I did not want began.

I was in the red six times in six months. The possibility of bankruptcy and foreclosure loomed in my future. And I created it!

I had a coach and I was unable to do what she suggested. I had put so much on my plate to prove myself that I was totally overwhelmed. I was so focused on other peoples' lack mindset that I created more lack in my life. Potential clients did not show up for consultations. Speaking engagements were cancelled. And I created it all! I was so stuck inside my head and desperately far away from my heart.

One morning a voice woke me up and asked, "Is it done time, Colleen? Are you done manifesting what you don't want and are you ready to manifest what you desire?" As I lay there in awe of what I heard, I put my hand on my heart and breathed slowly and intentionally, in and out. After a few minutes, I felt peace wash over me. With my hand still on my heart, I asked, "What do I need to know today? How can I be of service to others?"

That became my new routine before I got out of bed each day. And I embraced the quote by Khalil Gibran: "Faith is a knowledge within the heart, beyond the reach of proof."

As the days passed, I concentrated on keeping my home and growing my business. Any time fear or doubt started to creep into my mind, I stopped and put my hand on my heart and breathed.

Within a month I had a new sense of self-worth. Within six months other business entrepreneurs contacted me via email or LinkedIn to write articles and to do joint ventures with them. Previous clients signed up for more sessions. Potential clients scheduled consultations and I received speaking engagements.

The Universe is forever and totally Abundant. There is no lack except that which we create. As I let go of the thoughts that almost took me to financial ruination and incorporated more heartfelt thinking, I also let go of a relationship that was not healthy. While my boyfriend did things for me—drove me to and from the airport, watched my cats for me while I traveled, and even lent me money when I was at one of my lowest financial moments—there was no emotional support and we had nothing in common anymore. With the experience of new freedom, my thinking expanded and the abundance of the Universe entered into my life.

Colleen Humphries is an RN, Reiki Master, Author, and Certified Law of Attraction Life Coach guiding nurses and other professional women suffering from burnout that affects their lives mentally, emotionally, and physically. She helps them feel alive again and regain time for themselves and their families. www.colleenhumphries.com

It is precisely because we resist the darkness in ourselves that we miss the depths of the loveliness, beauty, brilliance, creativity, and joy that lie at our core.

– Thomas Moore

Betty Humphrey Fowler
Wounded Warrior

It's said that when life knocks you down, you just get up, dust yourself off, and get going again. No one ever tells you what to do when a huge hole in the ground swallows you up and you can't find your footing. That's what it feels like when someone you love develops an acute case of Post Traumatic Stress Disorder (PTSD). It covertly develops and takes years to work through. This is my story of how our family survived with little to go on but faith and trust.

Ever since he was five years old, my husband Wes dreamed of becoming a police officer. He wanted to follow in the footsteps of his cousin and lock up the bad guys and save people from having bad things happen to them.

Wes's professional training began after high school, working Security at a local department store. He signed up as an extra-help deputy for a Sheriff's Department in Southern California while he completed his Bachelor of

Arts degree in Criminal Justice. The arduous training at the Sheriff's Academy immediately followed, which culminated in Wes being sworn in as a deputy sheriff. He was finally performing what he knew was his true calling in life.

After working at the Sheriff's Department a few years, he transferred to a local city police department, where we met through a mutual friend. I was raised to respect and appreciate military and law enforcement personnel because they were there to help and protect us. But I had never known any police officers and had no idea what their lives were like.

Once we began a serious relationship, I went on many ride-alongs (being a passenger during a patrol shift) and saw first-hand the situations police encountered. I watched Wes and his fellow officers handle domestic violence calls, public intoxication, bar fights, runaways, and burglaries, and I was even involved in one police pursuit, chasing someone who had put another officer in physical danger. Fortunately, that chase ended without anyone being seriously hurt but, needless to say, it scared the "you-know-what" out of me! After that, I lost my desire to go on another ride-along. I did not want to repeat that anxiety.

I was always impressed with Wes's professionalism and focus during stressful and hostile situations. It takes a special kind of person to deal with encounters that most people avoid. I believe that police officers, along with our military, are heroes and warriors.

The truth about police work is that it is made up of many hours of mundane activity, broken up with moments of sheer adrenaline rush. There is no way to determine the types of calls coming in and, unfortunately, many can be emotionally difficult to handle afterwards. Wes was the first responder to countless calls that are forever etched in his mind: the murder/suicide of an entire family by the mother, SIDS deaths, suicides, child abuse cases, and horrific traffic accidents. When trauma is involved, emotional scars remain.

Wes handled these types of calls by putting his emotions aside and dealing with what needed to be done at the time. Those emotions were shoved behind a protective wall, like water being contained behind a dam. We did discuss what happened when he got home after each shift, but he held back major details to spare me any nightmares or worries. He wanted to protect me from everything that he witnessed.

I dealt with his work the best way I knew a cop's wife should. I prayed to God to protect Wes every time he left for work, and I put my faith and trust in his and the other officers' and dispatchers' training and their commitment to have each other's backs. I always focused on him being physically protected, but I never really considered his emotional vulnerability.

After several years in Southern California, we moved to Northern California. Wes began working at a city police department in the county next to ours, and he later became a sniper on their SWAT team. I had a dream job working as the head fitness instructor at the local Junior College Public Safety Training Center. We also added two children to our family. Life was working well for us for many years, until the dam started leaking. More incidents accumulated, including the suicide of my husband's training partner.

It was 25 years into his career, and 18 years into our marriage, when Wes handled a missing person call of a mother and her three-year-old daughter. While he was taking down information from the family, his dispatcher informed him that the mother had just walked into a hospital and turned herself in, confessing that she had killed the child and telling them where to find her.

Wes tried to maintain his professional demeanor, but the emotions from all of the other children's death calls he'd handled snowballed. He began crying when he made the death notification to family members. Then he couldn't stop crying and took the rest of the day off to recover. The following day at work he acted as if nothing out of the ordinary had happened, but I could tell something was not right. He was walking around in a zombie state. A few weeks later, we left for a week's vacation in Hawaii, but on the return flight, while coming into San Francisco, he had his first panic attack. He had his second as we drove through his work city on the way home. He told me that he couldn't handle another death call and he didn't know how he could survive as a cop. He never returned to work after that.

The response Wes received from his city and department was upsetting. The one time he needed support and help he was either ignored or shunned. Their attitude made me angry. I thought they would have had more concern for Wes's mental health since the suicide of his partner several years earlier. My anger and worry about Wes plunging deeper into depression, plus not being able to sleep through the night, kept me in a state of frustration and fear most of the time. I didn't know who I could trust or how to climb out of this black hole.

This was when I learned my first lesson in faith: Ask for help and expect to get it. I had no clue how to find the specific help Wes needed. His regular physician simply put him on meds to reduce his depression and blood pressure. I finally happened to mention our situation to an ex-dispatcher, whom we hadn't seen in months, who then notified a retired officer from Wes's department. The officer immediately jumped into action.

This "warrior angel," Mike, not only became a sounding board for Wes, but I could call him day or night if Wes was having a particularly hard time, and Mike would be right over. Mike understood Wes's situation, and he also had other resources at his disposal.

Mike got Wes enrolled in two one-week recovery retreats we'd known nothing about—The On-Site Academy in Gardner, Massachusetts and The West Coast Post-traumatic Retreat (WCPR), right in our own backyard. Wes was shipped off to On-Site first, then he attended WCPR right afterwards. He wasn't whole yet, but the healing had begun. WCPR had also just begun a program to help spouses work through their emotions, which I was able to attend. The first answer to both our prayers.

My second lesson in faith: Trust in others. Because the field of law enforcement is based on confidentiality, most people in that field keep things very private. Cops don't talk about issues that make them appear weak or a liability to other cops. It's a warrior trait and, understandably, PTSD is not a topic for open discussion. But there were those who did come out confidentially. Many fellow officers, who had gone through WCPR or On-Site, talked with Wes and shared their stories and offered support. Just knowing he wasn't alone was a tremendous help.

My third lesson in faith: Always believe that something good will come out of a difficult situation. Wes planned to retire at the end of a full career in law enforcement. He did receive his retirement, but it came five years early and with a disability. Not on the terms he expected. But what he went through guided him into a life filled with happier pursuits, such as more involvement with his kids, having better mental health, and becoming a Reiki practitioner. This warrior has turned into a healer, and now he has the chance to help others.

What helped us through much of this, besides the WCPR program, was using Feng Shui in our home. I had been reading about this ancient Chinese philosophy for a couple of years and now was determined to find out if it would shift Wes's depression.

I removed the clutter, thoroughly cleaned the house, and made sure it stayed clean. I kept Wes busy with a project he had started right before his breakdown—remodeling our kitchen. He was able to focus on doing something constructive, plus he knocked down a wall which created a better energy flow in the house. I bought a few healthy plants and kept them healthy. And I made sure our bed and the chairs Wes used situated him in a command position.

The Feng Shui principles I implemented were simple, yet effective in creating a healthy and safe environment for us to heal emotionally. We could now breathe deeply and think more clearly.

Wes's initial panic attacks and subsequent depression seemed insurmountable at first. But asking for help, trusting in others, and believing that things would change for the better allowed us to find a way to transform the negativity. Feng Shui was so instrumental in helping us through this challenging time that I became a trained consultant. It is such a wonderful feeling to live in a home that supports and protects you, even during the times you feel the most vulnerable.

F.A.I.T.H.

Betty Humphrey Fowler is a Feng Shui Consultant, Certified Interior Re-designer, author, speaker, and workshop presenter. She helps people transform their lives by improving the energy flow of their homes and work environments. Betty lives in the metro Atlanta area and offers private consultations, group presentations, and workshops. www.energizedspaces.com

When something happens, the only thing in your power is your attitude toward it; you can either accept it or resent it.

– Epictetus

SHERI BAGWELL
Open Heart

When I was a very little girl I was molested at the hands of my uncle. I was so young and confused that when he shamed me for being somewhere I was not supposed to be, I completely locked down and "forgot" what had happened to me. I wouldn't have had the language to talk about it anyway. Every time it happened again I was shamed for being in rooms I was not supposed to be in. That pattern led to a block in my brain, my body, and my energy field.

My body tried to talk to me about this when I was eight years old. I started vomiting every 28 days for two days. Everyone thought it was hormonally related, but I had not started my cycle so there was no way to treat me. People were confused. As the years went on the talk from my body got louder. I was in the hospital from pain and such profuse bleeding that I passed out. In my early teens I developed endometriosis (a much older person's disease) that led to surgeries and hormonal medications. None of that helped to cure the disease that was emotionally and energetically related.

When my mother or doctors would ask me if I had ever been molested or if anyone had touched me, I could not remember so I said "no." But my heart and my body knew the truth and I always felt like I was lying. Disconnected. I didn't know how to read my own body. I didn't know how to feel my heart. I had no trust of people. I harbored disgust, fear, and confusion. Frustration, anger, and sadness trapped themselves in my bones, muscles, and organs as well as the feeling that my body was not mine. I put a huge wall up around my heart to protect myself.

At 32 years old, a few months before I was supposed to have a hysterectomy, I found an energy healer. It felt like a miracle. Within three months of treatment my disease was gone. My energy was far more balanced. My body functioned much better than ever and I became happier.

There was still a bit of disconnect, though. My heart still had a huge wall. I would hear about people being able to read their bodies or go to their hearts for answers. I would ask questions and seem to get nowhere. So I started to commune with God and the angels through my brain. That worked only to a degree. I would get led in directions that were good for me, but there was still something unsettled. I was confused about that because I knew people that felt led by God in every moment and felt like they were complete, but I didn't feel complete. I didn't feel oneness.

Several years ago I found a program called "the emotion code." Through muscle testing you could find trapped emotions in your system and easily release them. You could find out if you had a heart wall and dismantle it. That was when the real healing of my soul started. That was when I began to be able to find my answers in my heart. Once the heart wall came down I became able to let my heart and my body lead me through my life.

That wasn't the end to my journey. Once I released the trapped emotions I was invited to an event where I was given the opportunity to look into the eyes of my abuser. And remember. As I looked in those eyes, I knew I had never been able to look in those eyes before. I allowed, without judgment, the hatred I had for him to rise from my pelvic floor and shoot out my eyes like lasers. I knew I was not afraid of him any longer. Now he was afraid of me. He cowered, his shoulders slumped, and he walked away like a guilty, bad dog.

The memories didn't actually come for a few weeks. The weeks and months that followed were a release like I had never experienced before. They were some of the most painful moments of my life. I cried the tears I was never given the opportunity to cry. I beat up pillows and my mattress to release the anger. I wrote letters that I never sent and one letter that I did send. Being able to look at everything in my system was such a relief. My bones, my muscles, and my organs vibrated with release. Heat rose from my body. Being willing to go into the pain, the fear, and confusion, and see it, experience it, love it, and thank it was what it really took for complete healing.

Once I dissolved my heart wall, one of the most fun and rewarding exercises that I found was to connect my heart with my mind. With that connection came peace and a deeper healing of the heart. I'd like to walk you through some exercises to help you make that connection.

Take a few deep breaths. Connect with my energy and allow the energy behind my written word to penetrate your body and being. As I ask you several questions, let your body feel the energy of the question and give you the "yes" that allows spirit to move through and change your energy.

"Am I willing to let a little piece of my heart wall dissipate?" Breathe that in . . .

"Heart, are you willing to let the wall come down completely?" Take a breath . . .

As you are more connected to your heart and more grounded to the earth you are always safe. You don't have to live in fear of what might happen. You will be aware of danger if it is close by. You can choose not to be around a person or you can choose to park in a different space or walk down a different road. When you let the illusion of fear go, there is nothing to be afraid of because you will be aware of danger. When you let fear go, you don't need the wall for protection. Breathe that in . . .

"Am I willing to open my heart to the universe of love waiting for me?"

All it takes is an opening. When you actually say "yes" the universe delivers more. Having the intention for the opening is what creates it. There is no ritual that you have to do. There are no special words that you have to say in any particular order. Just have an intention to allow your heart to open to the love from God or the Universe. Take a moment. Breathe that love in . . .

In the womb, the heart and mind sit right next to each other. As you grow, the heart and mind move farther apart. When you manage to connect the two there is a homecoming. There is a peace and stillness. Let me walk you through the process of reconnecting the two.

Connect to your thinking brain and pull that part of the brain into your heart. It usually moves slowly, especially the first few times. Sometimes it feels cramped at first, but that is just your heart healing your brain. Your heart reminds your brain about love and starts to dissipate anxiety. Keep with it. If your brain bounces out just bring it back. After a few times you will find that peace. The heart stills the mind and the mind will help bring more action to the heart's desires. To me it feels like a much more comfortable and loving place to operate from. It took some time to manage living here. I won't pretend that my mind lives in my heart all day every day. But the more I practice this, the easier it becomes.

If your brain gets to a place where you can't pull it down any farther, you can ask,

"What emotion is in the way of bringing my brain down into my heart?" and "What energy can I bring in to dissolve that emotion?"

These are the things that we learn from. These are the things that make us who we are. Without these experiences and release from them we would not be what we came here to be. I chose to be what I came here to be. I choose to be a light for others. I help women like myself and women who have experienced much worse release what is holding them back and connect with their hearts.

You have the ability to move energy to heal your own body. If you like the sound of these exercises and they make sense to you, but if you can't seem to make it work on your own, I highly recommend getting some help. Start by taking a guided meditation or a chakra class. Find an energy worker to walk you through some of these exercises. Move the stalled energy in your system to find a better life and body that works with you. When your heart and your mind are connected you will find a more sustained connection and happiness. There are ups and downs in life, and I won't pretend that you will never experience anything that makes you sad, but you will have the tools to allow the sadness and move back into joy.

Sheri Bagwell is a health and wellness coach and energy healer. She takes the life experience of healing her own body, combines that with knowing and ten years of expansive classes, and creates a personalized healing experience for her clients. www.sheribagwell.com

Do everything with a mind that lets go. Do not expect any praise or reward. If you let go a little, you will have a little peace. If you let go a lot, you will have a lot of peace. If you let go completely, you will know complete peace and freedom.

– Ajahn Chah

MICHELLE MECHEM
Freedom Through Detachment

As I sit down to write this, I hear the tap, tap, tap of a limb from a one hundred plus-year-old oak brush against my window in the breeze. It is an unusually cool day for Atlanta. The sky is grey through the eight-foot-tall casement windows. I can feel a draft through the single panes. Some of the glass is wavy and distorted, making the neighbor's home look more like a fun house. Every room bares a chalkboard halfway up the fourteen foot ceilings. My wood floors are weathered. I sometimes wonder how many tiny feet ran across them when this was a kindergarten and five streets over the first shots of the Battle of Atlanta were fired more than 150 years ago.

James Baldwin said, "Perhaps home is not a place but simply an irrevocable condition." I love this home, but it wasn't until I was able to get away from my attachment to it that I could truly live here.

F.A.I.T.H.

I started selling real estate in 2002. This is the fourth home I have owned. I bought my first at the age of 21. Having an interesting home is almost a requirement in my business, though most Realtors have the love of houses first. My neighbor was a successful photographer that dabbled in investment property. He owned a small percentage of a former Atlanta City school, and in 2004 he asked if I would take a look at it. He and his business partners had bought the entire elementary from the city in 1997 and turned it into 21 loft apartments. He was wondering if it made sense to convert them and sell them as condominiums. When I opened the door and walked up the stairs, I knew. Not only was it a good idea to convert these to condos, but I was going to buy the first one.

I was in the middle of a divorce after a three-year separation from my husband. This was a perfect space to renovate. Massive, light-filled, facing east, south, and west. I viewed it as the space for a new beginning. Number 4 never went on the market. A good friend and financial planner pointed out that in her business that was considered "insider trading." In mine it was just a perk. Not only did I have a great new space, I also had the income from selling the other twenty to fund my renovations. I had a blast. I designed a huge kitchen island with three different levels—low for rolling out dough, mid for chopping, and a high level for the seated bar. The marble company told me it was the largest single piece of granite they'd ever laid. I did everything I told my clients not to in a renovation. I painted bold colors and picked crazy patterned countertops. It was all me and my expression.

My business partner Hunter and I had formed the Hunter Group and our real estate business grew. We hired a full-time assistant and opened a stand-alone office in our neighborhood. We hired a Buyer's Agent. Life was good. In 2007 we started to hear murmurs from outside Georgia that the market was turning. But our business was still booming. Then in late 2007 the offices in the suburbs were saying their house sales were slowing. Still we were doing well. In March of 2008 the phones went quiet. We had ten people closing that month, but only two on the books for April. We assumed it was just a blip. We continued to generate leads and do everything we had always done to attract business.

We had to shift our business model. Home prices were rapidly dropping and many of the homes had higher mortgages than the market would bear. I learned a new skill in selling short sales. As mortgage companies failed we helped our customers by negotiating with the bank to get them out of their upside down loans. Our business continued but the profits dwindled. Soon I could see there was no money left to pay ourselves once the expenses were covered. I called my own mortgage company to ask for help. Their first question was, "Are you behind?" When I said no, I was refused help. I was stunned. Just because I wasn't behind now, I could see I would be in the coming months and I wanted a plan. I called back again and the answer was, "Don't call again unless you're behind."

I was raised with a high level of integrity, which meant paying your bills. So I began borrowing from credit cards, my retirement, and, as a last resort, family. The market was flat. I tried to find temporary work in my former profession. I had been a successful accountant when I left to start my real estate business. The harsh reality set in when the temp agency specializing in accounting told me they were placing CFOs in clerk positions. I had been out of accounting for seven years, so no one called. I stopped paying my mortgage.

At three months past due I started the loan modification process. I wrote a hardship letter, sent in financials, and waited. Three months later, the mortgage company sold my loan to another company and I had to start the process again. Nine months later that mortgage company went under and my loan was transferred yet again. I started getting pre-foreclosure notices and could feel myself panicking. I went to the dark place in my head. How was this going to look to the public? How could a real estate agent lose her own home? Not just an agent, but the agent who sold the 20 other homes in the building? Where was I going to live with no money and no credit? I pictured myself homeless, living in a box in Piedmont Park.

I caught myself on the edge of the deep dark abyss. My real estate business was still running. We didn't have the profit we wanted but we were still selling houses. My office had asked me to start coaching other agents. I had always been a positive force for others around me and now I needed to be it for myself. I had studied the Law of Attraction. At first I wondered what I had done to attract this mess. Then I asked a different question. What did I really want? I had heard a talk where a young woman was obsessed with reuniting with an old boyfriend. She shared that she visualized every day being with him and he still didn't love her. The speaker told her she was going about it the wrong way. There was nothing she could do to control the boyfriend; she could only control how she felt. So instead of being attached to being with him, she imagined how he had made her feel. Soon she met another man who was so wonderful she couldn't believe she had been so attached to the previous man. That was it! I was attached to my loft.

I gave up the attachment. Instead, I visualized feeling safe and secure. I visualized friends and family having dinner in my home. I saw everyone laughing. I went to bed at night not in a panic, but in peace, in the faith that I would have a home. I loved my home and still wanted to stay here, but I didn't have to. I opened to the possibility of something even better. Over five years my loft was slated to be sold on the courthouse steps four times. I wrote fourteen different hardship letters. I heard no, over and over, yet I stayed in action.

Then I received notice of an outcome from a class action lawsuit, and my second mortgage was released. $65,000 I no longer owed! Yet four months later I received another foreclosure notice on the first mortgage. I did what I could, and the Friday before the auction I got on a plane to head outside the country. I didn't know if my home would be sold while I was away. I received a voicemail that it was removed from the sale, but I did return to a letter stating they could not modify my loan. The mortgage company said they couldn't lower the payment by their guideline of 10%. I got back on the phone and told them they didn't need to. I made them an offer and they took it.

After five years of negotiating I got what I wanted—a lower mortgage, a lower payment, a low fixed rate, and no increase on the years of the loan.

Had I stayed attached to the idea that I had to live in *this* loft, I would have lost it. It is our feelings that pull us into the future. Instead of holding on to my fear, I focused on being safe, secure, and happy. I had faith that no matter where I lived I would have peace. The Universe decided it would be in a 114-year-old kindergarten.

Don't just visualize what you want, feel it. You can pull the future to you. Stay in action and do what you know to do. Live into it. The future is yours for the choosing.

Michelle Mechem is a Residential Realtor in Atlanta, Georgia and Partner in The Hunter Group at Keller Williams Intown. www.HouseHunterAtlanta.com. She specializes in Atlanta's Intown neighborhoods and the close-in suburbs. She is also a writer and Mentor/Coach for real estate agents. You can find her blog at www.ThrivingInRealEstate.com.

I believe that everything happens for a reason. Things go wrong so that you appreciate them when they're right. Sometimes, good things fall apart so better things can fall together.

– Marilyn Monroe

RANDI SHAPIRO

Under Fire

I wish I had understood Marilyn Monroe's way of thinking nearly 12 years ago, when my world came crashing down, after my own flesh and blood—my sister—fired me from the only job I ever wanted.

It was the Tuesday after Labor Day, 2002, and I was feeling refreshed after a four-day getaway at the beach in Destin, Florida with my husband. The drive in to work that morning was a beautiful one, and as I made my way along the hour commute all I could think about was what I needed to get accomplished once I got behind my desk. I was feeling extremely focused.

That clarity was soon shattered after I got out of my car and made my way down the sidewalk to my office. As I approached, there was my sister standing outside, blocking the door with a serious look etched on her face.

F.A.I.T.H.

"What's wrong?" I asked her uncomfortably, and she responded in a stern tone, "This is hard for me. I'm sorry, but I have to fire you."

Needless to say, I was numb. She explained she knew of an inappropriate business situation that I was involved in, and she felt she had no recourse but to take this action. I had no reason to believe she was aware of the situation, so I was stunned.

Our mother Marilyn had started and run the family recruiting business for almost 30 years before she passed away in March of 2000. Growing up I can still remember sitting down with her and my father as they would discuss her day at the office. I always knew I was a natural born sales person—I was always trying to sell somebody something! When I was about 20, I worked for a cosmetic company at a major department store where I would have to approach women and ask them to try products. I was great at it, but I knew I wanted more. I went to my mother and told her how I felt. She was happy I wanted to follow in her footsteps. My sister, nearly ten years older than I, had been working for the company for some time when I came on board. I started out in the front office as the receptionist and then at the age of 23 I began "working a desk" as my mother called it. My sister and my mother trained me—showed me the ropes.

I learned very quickly that recruiting was my true calling. I loved the business, and I loved helping people. Hearing how happy people were when I would make them a job offer was extremely gratifying—a true joy. There wasn't anything else I wanted or needed to do.

When Mom suddenly passed away I learned I had shares in the company though the majority shares of the company were left to my sister. In the end, I was fine with that as I did not want the responsibility and stress that went along with running a corporation.

I found out quickly that I was miserable working for my sister after my mother died. Initially, my sister and I collaborated on things; after a short time that changed. Mom had given me the latitude within reason to do what I wanted. She was happy with me as long as I was productive in my role with the company. In time, with my sister in charge, I felt as if I lost my sense of freedom. We didn't always see eye to eye and sometimes I had no real say in anything. It got to a point where I hated going to work most days, and on some mornings when I had severe distress, I would vomit before even leaving the house just from the very thought of how much I disliked working there. The passion and joy I once had for my job, and helping people, no longer existed.

So why was I so hurt and angry the morning I was fired? Yes, I did something I should not have done, and I realize now, many years later, I needed to take accountability for my actions. That day, I knew deep down I was absolutely responsible for my actions but wouldn't admit it. I just didn't care anymore about the job I had loved because I was so fed up and sad . . . and angry! The whole complexion of the company had changed without Marilyn. And I knew this in my core and in my heart.

So there I was, blindsided, and unceremoniously escorted off the property by security guards. My sister wouldn't even let me back inside my office that day to gather items that were important to me.

I couldn't believe that this was happening, and I started to become frantic. My head felt like it was going to explode with all of the emotions I was feeling. When I got back into my car—which only minutes before had been a place full of optimism and hope—I sat and wept uncontrollably before I could get myself together to call my husband and tell him what had occurred.

As I drove back home crying, I couldn't help but feel like I was going through another death in my family. I remember constantly thinking in disbelief, "My own sister did this to me."

When I finally got back home, my husband was there to greet me with a gigantic hug. As he wiped away some more of my tears, he looked into my eyes, and in a calm, cool, collected voice said the words that never even entered my mind, "Randi, this could be the best thing that ever happens to you!"

And he was right. As was my best friend, who basically said the same exact thing.

My sister gave me a *great gift*. She *truly* did. I just didn't know it on *that* day and for some time really years afterwards.

So, there I was, trying to figure out what I was going to do. My mother had owned her reputable employment agency for 30 years and everyone in the recruiting industry knew I was her daughter. How was I going to get a job? What firms or other staffing agencies were going to hire me? That consumed me day and night.

I decided to reach out to colleagues and contacts that my mother knew. A couple of weeks passed, and through those contacts I happened on to several women who helped me realize that I could go out on my own and start my own recruiting firm. They shared information about a group of professionals that all had their own independent recruiting firms which helped each other in placing candidates seeking employment with companies. They instilled in me that I could do anything I put my mind to, and it was simply up to me to make it happen.

While I was hesitant about the thought of joining them at first, I knew I had to do it. Nervous and excited, I knew I had to go out on my own! Just one month after getting fired, I started my own company. It was bittersweet in the very beginning, though it taught me that getting fired by my sister forced me to find the "real" me. It made me a stronger person.

Ever since I was a young girl I always felt I needed approval, whether it be from my mother, my father, and yes, even my sister! But through the experience of what happened that day in 2002 and since, I have come to the realization that the only approval I need is *my* approval!

With guidance and counsel from my peers and others I was given faith and hope and, as a result, I transcended the pain and the anger. These wonderful women were, and still are, an integral part of the person I have become today—a successful business woman who lives her life leading from the heart. I now go through life with the faith in who I am and what I believe in, and the gratitude in knowing that anything in life is possible.

It hasn't always been easy. Twelve years later there are still hard times. And I have learned that leading from my heart, letting go, believing in myself personally and professionally, and being grateful for everything I have is the reason I have persevered.

When I share my story with candidates who are seeking new careers, I hope they realize I can commiserate with them. With great compassion I listen to their stories about being laid off, fired, or having their positions eliminated. When I receive calls from candidates who tell me about losing a job, I tell them I've been through all of the emotions that go along with it. That I truly understand.

But over and above anything else, with a big smile on my face, and a slight giggle in my voice, I tell them the most important thing they need to know: "Everything happens for a reason, and this could be the best thing that ever happens to you!"

After all, it was for me. Thanks to my sister.

Randi Shapiro founded Recruiting Specialists Inc., a national staffing and recruiting firm located in Atlanta, Georgia, in 2002. She prides herself on delivering top talent to small, medium, and Fortune 500 companies, is very passionate about her craft, and adores building relationships with both the clients and candidates she serves. www.recruitingspec.com

Faith is to believe what you do not see;
the reward of this faith is to see what you believe.

– Saint Augustine

LINDA MINNICK

Just Listen

I've been hearing a voice in my head since I was little. I wasn't ever frightened by it. I realized it was part of me. It didn't speak all the time, only when it needed to. I can also get pictures of myself and others in the future. I use these pictures as confirmations.

When I was young I could see a picture of myself graduating high school and I would get a feeling of satisfaction. Graduating from high school I could look ahead and see myself at 27. The pictures never showed me many details. All I could see was that I was still around and healthy!

I used this gift of pictures each time I was pregnant. If I could see my child accepting his or her diploma while being called the name we had picked out, I knew the name was right. As my children grew, whenever I was worried about them I would close my eyes and ask for pictures of them in the future. When I saw them as adults, I would know that they would be fine.

These visions threw me with my oldest son. When he was young, I asked for pictures of his future. I could see him through the age of 19, then not again until he was 29. The voice that had been with me since childhood explained what this meant. I knew it was true because the voice was always true. I didn't want to believe it nor did I have to until that night, at the age of 19, when he made the decision to leave.

The calm, inner voice had given me a heads up that morning. It told me that an argument between us would be the vehicle he would use to make his exit. I spent the day telling myself I could control the situation. Whatever happened, we wouldn't argue. I would keep my mouth shut. But I didn't. When he came home hours late to a family dinner party I calmly asked where he had been. That was the only question that came out calmly. Like reading our lines from a script, we began our volley of words and emotions. We locked eyes for just a moment and I heard his voice in my head say "goodbye." Forcing myself to stop and hoping to change the outcome, I grabbed my keys and left the house. By the time I returned, he was gone.

For years I walked around in a fog. I quit my job. I gained over thirty pounds. I cried on a daily basis. Every day I questioned the parenting choices I had made for him and was making for the other three children still at home. Would they leave too? It took two years to accept what the voice had been telling me the entire time. He was on his own path and I did not control the Universe or my children. The visions told me he would return. They showed him with a beautiful little boy with ringlets of gold. He did return and my grandson's name is Fletcher.

The visions seem to be pretty selective about what they would show me. I never got a vision about who I would marry. So I never saw John, my husband. His appearance into my life came out of left field. He wasn't anything like anyone I had dated before. My taste had always been blue collar guys. I didn't go looking for these types. I just happened to live in a blue collar neighborhood. Not John.

John was a senior at Washington University, one of the most recognized engineering schools in the country. He was incredibly smart, played several instruments, and spoke with the voice of liquid honey. He had beautiful red hair, sparkling blue eyes, a great body, a kiss that would melt an iceberg, and the sense of humor of a science teacher. John and I really didn't have a whole lot in common but that didn't seem to matter. For whatever reason we were attracted to each other and, like most young adults at that stage, we spent as much time as possible with each other. A few weeks into our relationship that still, small voice in my head said "you're going to marry him."

I didn't appreciate this announcement. I had just spent the last three years of my life managing the family home while my mom had been ill. As a high school student, my life was filled with grocery shopping, cooking, cleaning, laundry, plus school. By the time I graduated from high school, Mom was on the upswing. When I met John, I was just at a point where my responsibilities were beginning to subside. I was not ready to go from running one house to having to run another.

Yet the voice was right again. Ten months into the relationship our days were pretty much intertwined. After graduating from college, John's new job transferred him out of state. We felt we couldn't live without each other and decided to get married. Fifteen months after I heard the voice, we were moving out of state together.

In the first ten years of our marriage, we had moved four times with John's job, ending in Atlanta. All said and done, we added two sons and two daughters to the mix. Like all young families, our days were filled with laundry, schedules, work, bills, laundry, emergencies, school . . . and, did I mention, laundry?

By this time, I recognized that the voice was normally right. So I learned to pay attention when it spoke. It helped me as I traversed the path of mother, wife, and woman, but I pretty much ignored it when it came to my career. I knew in high school my career was to be one of service, to get paid helping people understand the greatness within and be the best they could be.

Other than doctor or nun, there was no title to put on a career like that in 1972, especially for a woman. As I had no interest in either of those professions, I ignored the voice for years. But with each new job I started, the voice would always ask, "So how exactly are you helping people here?" I thought I appeased the voice somewhat when I got into sales and training. But it would say, "You need to go farther." Instead, I used excuses such as "I'm too busy raising a family" or "I don't have the education" . . . or whatever.

Several decades later, things finally erupted. In 2009 I had everything I thought I wanted. I had four wonderful adult children, a wonderful husband, a nice home, a good job with a great salary, and I was miserable. All of the excuses I had used over the years to avoid doing what my soul wanted to do weren't holding water any more. They were leaking all over my life! My misery grew until I finally hit a wall. It felt like the world was collapsing underneath me. My still, quiet voice was now demanding to be heard. "It's time," it said. "*Now!*" So after trying to fight it for a year, I surrendered. "God, show me how," I pleaded. And He did.

Within days of that desperate prayer people started showing up in my life. One person asked me the pivotal question, "Why aren't you coaching?" When I heard that, every nerve ending in my body screamed "That's it!" and I knew my life had changed. Since there were no more excuses, there was no ignoring the voice.

It's been years since then. I've studied, worked, and expanded my knowledge and experiences. I've coached and presented on stages across the country. I have seen the joy in the eyes of my clients as they wake up to realize their true potential. And the biggest lesson I've learned is one that was presented to me years ago. Listen. Listen to the voice. Pay attention to the visions. These are gifts of the Spirit. These are your guiding lights.

I have to admit my life has never been happier than it is right now. I wake up every morning thanking God for helping me recognize that I can have a professional career in serving others and I go to bed thanking God for each opportunity I had to serve. I realize by trying to be the best I can be, and helping others to be the best they can be, that I am helping the Universe be the best it can be. That every time one of my clients reaches a new level of joy and fulfillment, the world is a better place.

I know without the experiences I've had in my life, I wouldn't be the person I am today. It took a while to get here but I've arrived. And while I'm still learning, I am glad to be alive! I'm so glad I have learned to listen, listen with my ears, my heart, and my being. So glad to finally be living the life I was meant to live.

Linda Minnick is a certified life coach, speaker, PSYCH-K® Facilitator, and a specialist in transformational thinking. She helps her clients ignite the potential within them to attain the results they have been looking for, and she gives them the tools to continue on that upward spiral of fulfillment and success.
www.lindaminnick.com

Sometime in your life you will go on a journey. It will be the longest journey you have ever taken. It is the journey to find yourself.

– Katherine Sharp

Rude Awakening

I hadn't slept for three straight days. I'd never been a good sleeper, but I couldn't remember a time in my life when I'd gone more than a day without some sleep. But there I sat at my computer emailing a coworker's guru for help.

"I have to warn you . . . I'm a basket case," I typed. Within an hour, the brief response caused tears of hope to roll down my cheeks.

"Basket cases are my specialty," she responded to my desperate plea.

Just a year earlier was a very different, more familiar life—the top biller for a nationwide recruiting company with a beautiful home, luxury car, and making more money than I'd ever dreamed was possible. I'd always known what I wanted back then and it was money. Money would buy me freedom and happiness. Coming from a blue collar family and hearing the repeated "money doesn't grow on trees," I'd wanted to break free of the "lack" consciousness.

I don't recall what happened first, my mother finding out she had stage five melanoma cancer or realizing money wasn't buying me anything that mattered. Most certainly it wasn't buying me happiness and the family I'd always wanted. In addition, I took many daily medications and was frequently sick with gall stones, a heart defect, asthma, tons of dental work, chronic sinus infections, eating disorder, endometriosis, and frequent laryngitis.

I'd also given up on having an intimate relationship after I dated the same guy in many different bodies throughout my twenties. And I was the Queen of repressing emotions. I hadn't cried in over ten years!

When my mother found out about the softball-sized tumor on her spinal cord, I decided to research, learn, and help manage her process. The oncologist estimated she had one to two years. She lived only six more weeks. Those six weeks changed my life and were the catalyst for the scariest year of my adult life.

My mother had always battled with constant physical and emotional pain. Even though our lives appeared to be very different on the outside, we had similar paths. Growing up, there was no religion or spirituality in our home. There simply wasn't enough worthiness in our house to have a relationship with God.

During the last chapter of my mother's life, I was a student of her releasing process and her last-ditch attempt to feel worthy of going to heaven. What a relief to be present when she would speak of conversations with people on the other side. Then she would catch herself and say, "Oh, how could I have been talking with them? They died years ago." But I was so grateful to find out that there indeed was another side and that when she passed she would be met by those who cared about her.

This newfound knowledge and awareness transformed me and I threw myself into learning more about spirituality. Upon returning home, I was saddened to find out my kitty, Khalua, had advanced colon cancer. Weeks after my mother's passing, I had to say goodbye to my beloved, beautiful calico. It was gut wrenchingly painful, unlike any pain I'd felt before in my forty years. She was hands down the greatest teacher of love in my life. She was the first soul to pry open my heart and it was breaking.

My mother wasn't a cat lover so I was concerned there'd be no one to greet Khalua on the other side. So I sat in my bedroom crying and pleading for God or angels to be there for her so she wouldn't be alone. Then through my sobbing I said, "Just let her come back and live here with me!"

Khalua had always been a very routine cat. Every night when I went to bed, and I mean every night, I turned off my light, turned on my side, then I felt the thump of her jumping on the bed by my feet. She would walk up the bed to my pillow where she waited for me to lift the covers so she could get warm and cozy behind my knees.

The first night after Khalua passed I held my breath as I felt that same thump on the bed, then the pressure of a cat walking up the bed to my pillow. I jumped up and quickly turned on the light. No cat . . . there was nothing. This happened several nights in a row. Then I actually began to see Khalua. Really see her soul and feel her rub against me too. In those first weeks she would show up at all of her regular places doing her routine things. It brought me such peace knowing she was still with me.

Soon afterwards, my newly acquired sixth sense morphed to seeing into other dimensions. That's when it got scary. Not only was I seeing Khalua, but also my mom, and tons of other unfriendly male souls that I didn't know and didn't want to know. Long repressed childhood memories were coming to life and being reenacted to me, memories of physical, emotional, and sexual abuse. I was petrified. Names of my abusers were given to me, actual names of men in my home town, like the janitor at my elementary school who had been terminated due to sexual molestation of children. The most terrifying and shocking memories revealed were from a group of men my mother was associated with during the first years of my life.

No matter what I tried, I couldn't turn off the constant energetic attacks. They were worse at night, mirroring the time of the most intense abuse during my childhood. Lights were turning off and on, my house smelled like cigarette smoke even though I'd never smoked, and my body would vibrate with the energy jumping in and out of it. The few friends I confided in tried to be supportive but it was a lot for anyone to understand. Not once did I question my sanity. These experiences were real. The logical part of me just wanted to find a way to get control. Repressing my emotions was no longer an option. I cried, screamed, fought, and was pissed off. And the thing that scared me the most was going to sleep.

The desired turning point came through a conversation at work with a very close and respected friend. After I shared what I'd been going through she calmly said, "There's something I am having a hard time understanding. If you are tapping into all of this negative stuff, why aren't you able to tap into anything positive, specifically . . . God?"

When I left work that evening, I couldn't get her question out of my head. Why *hadn't* I been able to tap into God or see anything good? As I approached a stoplight, a homeless man walked up to the window of my car. I'd never given money to a homeless person. It wasn't a behavior that felt safe. But without even thinking, I put my window down and grabbed my purse. I didn't have much cash but I gave him what I had. He smiled sincerely and said, "God loves you!" I quickly raised my head to meet his eyes and immediately felt his warmth and love, as if he looked straight through me and saw the real me. With a lump in my throat I managed to ask, "Are you sure?" Without hesitation his grin grew larger and there was a glint in his eye as he responded, "Of that, I be sure."

The entire drive home I cried, and cried, and cried some more. I then understood I had never let God, or anyone else, help me due to a belief that no one was safe. All of my life, through all the loneliness, pain, and shame, I never once trusted or believed that anyone would love me unconditionally except for my pets.

In that moment I realized that protecting myself from the bad had also kept out the good. When I arrived home, still sobbing, I looked to the ceiling and exclaimed, "I get it. I realize I haven't let you help me!" Then I watched, with splendor and awe, the gift of a lightshow filled with spectacular colored confetti and angels that I will forever remember. Tears of joy and relief were endless that evening, and angels blanketed me as I slept all night.

Within a week, I began seeing an energy healer. She helped me to begin healing the decades of fear, pain, and shame that I had carried with me since childhood. I'll never forget how much better I felt directly after the first session. It was amazing! No doctor or drug had so gently and lovingly brought me to this place of feeling like . . . me. In that instant I told her, "I want to do what you do."

I delved into a very deep healing journey for many years. It was far from easy, but I saw such value in it every step of the way because of how much better I felt. My physical ailments healed and there was no longer a need for any medication.

Having awareness of my painful past made it easier to allow in love, nurturing, and compassion for myself. I also embraced a new path of getting certified in bioenergetics so I could begin helping others to transform their lives.

Every single pet, person, and experience has guided me to heal, evolve, and love at deeper levels, and in turn help others to feel more love and create the lives they've dreamed of. Everyone deserves to be loved and to thrive! It takes a lot of courage to look at the wounds and pain that binds us, but each step of the way is worth it to feel more joy and love every single day.

Tammy Billups is a Certified Bioenergetics Therapist and founder of Sundance Healing Center. She has facilitated thousands of sessions and is honored to work with both two- and four-legged souls, knowing this miraculous holistic healing modality can significantly enhance lives. www.tammybillups.com

It's a funny thing about life; if you refuse to accept anything but the best, you very often get it.

— Somerset Maugham

Ricia L. Maxie
Great Expectations

My spirit soared with a sense of newfound freedom and simultaneously I felt a bit unsure and anxious when my husband, children, and I moved from the wine country in Sonoma County. It was 1986 and I had never lived outside a thirty-five mile radius.

Life in my youth had been one of certainty with few unexpected changes. As a young adult, my life transformed to one of uncertainty and constant change but frequently without overwhelming fear due to trust in Guidance. (The term Guidance is used interchangeably with the term Divine, which provides heavenly and spiritual insight.) Each one of my encounters with Guidance helps me strengthen my trust and reduce my fear.

Born and raised in the lush, tree-laden Marin County (immediately north of San Francisco and the Golden Gate Bridge), I was 26 when my husband and I moved north of Marin to Rohnert Park, Sonoma County, to purchase our first home. We lovingly referred to Sonoma County as Marin North since half of my friends and most of my family had moved there to purchase more affordable housing. The wine country was beautiful at every viewpoint with vineyards, apple orchards, and plum trees filling the open land. Of course, that wasn't to last long with the housing boom that was taking off. Not letting moss grow under our feet, we bought and sold twice after that to be able to house our growing family in a home that fit us more comfortably with plenty of bedrooms, bathrooms, living areas, and an oversized kitchen.

We settled into our home and routine for a couple of years while I was employed with a quasi-government agency with whom I had fully intended to retire. My husband had been pursued by an organization that admired his work and offered him a position that held much promise. So it was a complete surprise when, within two weeks of each other, we were both let go. After a few weeks of our release, my father moved in; he was dying of cancer and we provided full-time care for the last six months of his young life.

Two years after my father's premature death, we sold the house and moved to a rental further north at the edge of the Redwoods on five acres overlooking a vineyard which was within a quarter mile of a small lake. The property felt sacred; we meditated daily, visited often by Guidance.

Life changed again when my husband secured a position in Sunnyvale after just one year on this idyllic property. This was the move outside my geographic comfort zone, away from my family of origin, yet the new adventure brought excitement with new roads, new friends, and life in a community that was incredibly fast-paced. At times I believed that no one in this community slept.

After one year in Sunnyvale, we had to make a decision on an approaching deadline: pay capital gains tax on the house we sold or buy a home and close the loan before the two-year time period elapsed. That cut-off date was looming only two months away.

During tax season, our accountant advised us to pay the capital gains tax up front, insisting that there was no way we could find a home and close within two months. He was feeling an urgency to be proactive. My husband and I looked at each other and almost in unison stated that we'd be able to purchase and finalize a deal on a home before the due date. Although the accountant insisted, we felt confident that Guidance would lead the way and direct our search.

Every morning, my husband and I meditated for at least twenty minutes. Sometimes I would verbally guide the meditation, sometimes he would guide, and every now and then we would both be silent. We both felt Guidance's presence and thus continued to feel inspired on a daily basis.

During the first month of the two-month deadline, we would see our new house in our minds. It would have at least three bedrooms and two bathrooms and would be in a safe and lovely neighborhood. Our meditation technique also called for us to actually experience what it was like to be in our own home again, feeling the elation signing the papers, moving in our furniture, cooking our meals. We could almost smell the food being prepared in the kitchen, the incense burning in the living room, the scent of burning candles on the table in the room in which we would meditate. The sounds of laughter and chatter from family members would waft through the rooms in the house, especially noisy at Christmas as we all surrounded the Christmas tree in its appropriate space.

Each day we would add to the meditation and each day we would feel the energy of the home surround us more strongly. And every day, the images, feelings, and sounds would be released to the Divine in an imaginary bubble that would float up into the Light. We knew the Divine would assist us in whatever direction was right for us. There were no strings attached. On one hand, we knew that we'd get a house and close within the necessary time frame, and yet, on the other hand, we weren't attached to an outcome. This may sound like an oxymoron but that ease of creating and letting go of the creation was real. There's a fine line to desiring an outcome and letting go of the attachment to it. By letting go, something even better could possibly be created.

In the mid-80's, loans for house sales were backed up and took four to six months to close, at best. Interest on home loans was enormously high but for some reason people had an itch to buy. This created a booming economy but also made it difficult to work through the lengthy financing timeline. We knew we wanted to move back to Sonoma County and my husband had been promised a transfer, so we chose the Fourth of July holiday weekend to scour the area for a house. We packed up our family and some snacks and headed north for a day trip. During the two-hour drive we stopped for gas and I happened to pick up a free, newspaper quality real estate guide listing homes for sale all over the San Francisco Bay area. While scanning the listings, I noticed the perfect house in Santa Rosa just a few miles north of where we bought our first home.

We called the realtor to let him know we were only up for the day; he left the barbeque he was attending to show us the house an hour later. It was perfect: a cute, white house in an older, established neighborhood with three bedrooms and two bathrooms, a galley style kitchen, and mature fruit and nut trees on the property. The lot had good-sized back, side, and front yards with a curved driveway. The floors were in beautiful shape and the layout of the rooms was exactly what we needed at the time even though each room needed a fresh coat of paint. The landscaping was overgrown and mostly dead, but given all of the pluses and minuses, the property was a great price, especially considering the housing prices at the time. The homeowner was even willing to finance the loan so no need to wait for a lengthy closing period through the bank. And since the realtor was also an attorney he drew up the necessary papers. Each person involved had integrity with a willingness to work together toward a win-win-win outcome. We moved within thirty days!

When we called our accountant to give him the good news he told us it was impossible to have completed a deal; he just couldn't hear that the deal was completed and continued to insist that we file for capital gains. Later when we showed him the paperwork he was utterly speechless and repeatedly shook his head in amazement.

Guidance has always steered us in the right direction and when we trust and let go miracles happen. There were so many opportunities to learn from this experience: we may not always understand why things happen when they do but we learned that it's always right timing where Guidance was concerned even if the situations seem devastating, I could move to a new city and discover my inner independent spirit, and my husband and I could release all doubt and totally trust in Guidance, the Divine.

Ricia L. Maxie, M.A., is an internationally renowned intuitive consultant/mystic, Reiki practitioner, and speaker and has been providing intuitive consultations, leading spiritual retreats, and teaching classes and meditation for thirty years.
www.ricialmaxie.com

Your task is not to seek for love, but merely to seek and find all the barriers within yourself that you have built against it.

— Rumi

LAINA ORLANDO

Third Time's a Charm

"I do!" I exclaimed joyfully when the minister asked if I would take the beautiful man standing before me as my wedded husband.

The night sky was clear, and the crisp October temperature was perfect for the outdoor celebration of our legal union. As our family and dearest friends gathered around us, the luminous glow cast by some fifty overhead Chinese lanterns set the stage for the enchanting evening. This magical night marked the start of our married life.

Once again, I became a wife. And once again, for the third time, I thought to myself, what the hell have I done?

During my previous two marriages, the first at seventeen and the next at twenty-four, I was determined to show my husbands just how strong, confident, and powerful I was. I made it clear that I wasn't going to stick around unless I was in charge of the show; I meant the marriage. So both relationships started off without a hitch.

I entered into my first holy matrimony just a few weeks after we both graduated from high school. While my heart made it clear I was in love, my head buzzed with plans to secure my future. After bouncing between four different foster families in dysfunctional homes, over the previous two years, I was determined to start a stable family life of my own. I was itching to settle down and shower my beloved with my idea of true love, the kind I had desperately yearned to experience years before.

My parents divorced when I was only ten years old, leaving me with a clear idea of the missing ingredient for happiness: that to love is to give, since that was the one thing I don't remember witnessing. So I was determined to be an excellent giver of love.

Once the newness of unchaperoned dates and sex-on-demand wore off, my husband and I quarreled about our different perspectives on love and marriage. I believed in giving my all, which included my love and my know-it-all opinions, but I wasn't interested in receiving his in return. It wasn't long before my approach left me feeling rejected, misunderstood, and packing my bags. After we divorced at the ripe old age of 19, the voice in my head simply sighed, "Poor guy, he simply couldn't handle all I had to give."

At 24, I felt I was ready to give marriage another try. This time, my heart was aflutter for a fella that shared my passion for starting a family. One year and two days into our marriage, I became a mother. With my own child's happiness at stake, the voice in my head commanded me to take control of the marriage. My head rationalized that my new family deserved to receive all of the love and attention I had to give. As long as I was busy giving I felt fulfilled.

For 23 mostly wonderful years, I poured my heart into my family, even though the voice in my head whispered, "What about me? Who's taking care of me?" Deep inside I was tired of my role of giver. I was tired of being strong and in control. Yet the fear of failure and divorce kept me looking for ways I could make things better. But the day inevitably came to transition our marriage back to our original friendship.

My third marriage came bearing the gift that rocked my perception about love.

I was 48 and wiser. The instant our eyes met we each felt a deep soul mate connection, like a remembering that we had already known and loved each other before. It was truly magical, unlike anything I had ever experienced. I was instantaneously and deeply in love.

From the start of our relationship, my beloved and I were head over heels for each other. I had never felt so effortlessly received, and cherished, for exactly who I was. I freely, and joyfully, gave my love, my wisdom, and myself. And as he kept coming back for more, I happily gave and gave. Feeling received by him made me feel safe, loved, and special.

Soon after the wedding vows were shared, the insidiously familiar fear cropped up. As my beloved showered me with his love, his abundance, and his wisdom, the voice in my head began to whisper, "Watch out. If you take more than you give you'll be trapped." Although we adored each other, I felt afraid that I would become controlled and powerless. It soon became clear that we had entered into a giving competition, with each of us believing that our own offerings were more valuable.

The old familiar thoughts consumed way too much space in my head and my desire to clearly see what was happening brought me into deep self-inquiry. I needed to know why our relationship had shifted so dramatically. And I became aware that neither of us was comfortable receiving. Needless to say, when there are two givers and no takers, love is left unclaimed.

The wisdom I had acquired, thus far, came through my being aware of the difference between the voices in my head and the voice of my heart. My head always instilled fear, while my heart engendered only love. As I inquired into the discomfort I felt in receiving my beloved's love, I realized I gave love as a form of protection. As a ten-year-old child, I witnessed my parents not giving their love to each other, but it never occurred to me that maybe, just like me, they, too, were afraid to receive.

Listening to the voice of my heart showed me that I had to ignore my head's insistence that I bolt. I was deep into

THIRD TIME'S A CHARM

my spiritual journey, and running away in fear was simply not an option. Although my head promised that I would find freedom by leaving, my heart reminded me that to love, and be loved unconditionally, is true freedom.

Guided by faith, I probed my fear of opening up and receiving love without needing to justify my worth. During my first two marriages I truly believed the voice in my head which said, "Give, give, give, and they won't leave you." What I most wanted as a child was for my parents to give me their love, so I could feel special, worthy, and secure. I concluded that the giver of love held all of the power, and the one longing to receive was destined to suffer, as I did. Therefore, I entered into relationships with the belief that, through giving, I could prove I was worthy of receiving another's love. It wasn't until my third marriage that I realized giving to get is always based on fear, because it reinforces the belief that I was unworthy.

In a moment of silent clarity, my heart whispered, "Open up and receive." After a lifetime of giving love to feel safe and in control, receiving love, without having to somehow pay for it, felt needy, raw, and vulnerable. Giving numbed the discomfort of feeling empty, unworthy, and abandoned by my parents. But my heart was instructing me to open up to receive the gift of love simply because I exist.

Faith in the power of love gave me the strength to question the voices in my head so I could shift my outdated and insane belief about love. I realized that unconditional love is a sign of strength since it asks for nothing in return. And I discovered that in the act of receiving another's love, I experienced the joy of sharing my love without condition.

I felt deep gratitude that the blocks to my receiving love could finally be seen and released. I became aware that all along, love had been waiting for my welcome of it.

Once I made the conscious choice to open up and receive my beloved's love, without having to do a damn thing in return, I finally acknowledged my wholeness, worthiness, and my magnificence. Love had been with me all along. Through the patience and the kindness of the whispers of my heart, I am now open to claiming all of love's infinite gifts.

Marriage offered me three opportunities to discover that receiving love is far more courageous than giving love. Now I recognize that unconditionally receiving another's love is an act of self-love. By receiving my husband's love, regardless of how it is offered, I am acknowledging my worthiness and wholeness. And in return, my loving gratitude is the sweetest gift I could ever give him, because it affirms the magnificence of the love he is offering to me.

No longer do I allow the voice of fear to cause me to discard love as a form of protection. My heart has awakened me to the truth that I am, as is he, the delicious expression of love personified. The greatest gift I could ever offer another is my recognition that we are all naturally worthy of loving and being loved. Giving and receiving come from a whole and worthy heart overflowing with love.

I am eternally grateful that I chose to listen to the truth my heart has been whispering to me all along. The third time truly is a charm!

Laina Orlando loves simplifying spirituality for today's seekers of truth. As an author, speaker, coach, and creator of The Power of Awareness program, Laina's techniques, humor, and timeless wisdom transform weighty spiritual concepts into practical bite-sized morsels that can be easily practiced in everyday life. Her mantra: Life is fun and easy! www.lainaorlando.com

Your vision will become clear only when you can look into your own heart. Who looks outside, dreams; who looks inside, awakes.

– Carl Jung

Nanette Littlestone
Trust Me!

When I was six years old I asked God to kill me.

No, I wasn't crazy. And yes, six years old is a little young to want to die. But I didn't really want to die. I just wanted to understand the concept of God. My parents weren't religious. We didn't go to temple (we're Jewish), we didn't read the Old Testament, and we didn't talk about the evils of sin or the goodness of prayer. We didn't even talk about God.

I decided to put God to the test. If he was real, I would die. If he wasn't real, I would go on living.

That night I prayed for the real God to show himself.

I woke up the next morning and realized my wish hadn't come true.

Why didn't I die? If God was real, I would have died.

God let me down.

There was only one conclusion. God was not real.

F.A.I.T.H.

Granted, I was only six, but disappointment settled over me like a heavy coat. I couldn't see it, but I could feel its weight. I'd wanted to believe in something and that something was yanked away from me.

So I stopped believing.

Two years later, in third grade, my mother told me I had hurt a child's feelings during class. My teacher didn't tell me directly. She informed my mother that I had committed this crime and my mother now had to relay the news to me. My mother probably suggested that I watch what I say and do my best not to hurt anybody else's feelings. But that's not what I heard. I heard, "You hurt somebody. Don't do that again."

I was already shy growing up and didn't talk much, even to my friends. When I did speak, I said what I felt. I didn't know that was wrong. Now my mother was telling me that my words were weapons. I could hurt somebody with words. Opening my mouth was harmful.

That was the day I shut down. If someone spoke to me I spoke back. I had conversations with my friends and family. But I took great care never to hurt someone with my words. If no one asked for my opinion, I kept it to myself. If someone did ask, I made sure I said something nice.

I didn't realize this simple belief would kill my self-esteem.

Those two childhood experiences shaped my destiny. I went out into the world protected with impenetrable armor and a lack of trust, ready to battle anyone and everyone. Life ambled along quite well, I thought. I had good jobs, I met interesting people, I traveled, married a wonderful man, found my passion—writing. But something inside was restless. I wanted more, bigger, better. Not necessarily cars and houses and money, although I love those things. It went deeper. More personal.

My soul was calling.

Several years ago I was thinking about God, love, the oneness that connects us all, the dips and turns and erratic bends of my spiritual journey, and I was wondering how I/we make sense of it all. An angel whispered "F.A.I.T.H. – Finding Answers in the Heart." My spirit rose on a familiar wave of joy. Then my mind took over and began to analyze. *What a great title. I wonder what I can do with it. Maybe I could write about my own journey.* Then my good friends Doubt and Worry appeared. *Why would anyone want to read about you? You're not famous. You have to be famous to write a book. This is stupid.*

So I shelved the idea.

Life went on.

My soul kept calling.

I don't like change. Doubt and Worry do their best to shelter me from proactive thinking, and Resistance makes sure I don't move too fast. When crazy ideas pop into my head, my "friends" investigate and scrutinize and analyze things to death, just to protect me from doing something that might be a little uncomfortable. It's always easier to remain in a place I know than to venture out somewhere new.

But my soul had other ideas. What I didn't understand as a child is that we are spiritual beings having a human experience. We're here on Earth to learn what it is to be human. To laugh, to cry, to feel pain, to feel joy. And the lessons are repeated until we understand them, until we have that "knowing" in our hearts. I was hurt as a child. My trust was broken. Now it was time to heal.

This time the voice whispered "F.A.I.T.H." and "partnership." A collaborative book. Multiple authors gathering together to write on the same subject from different points of view. A perfect blend of my idea with a collection of inspiring stories. How exciting! My own faith blossomed.

I mentioned my idea to Mindy Strich, my energy healer, and felt that inner tingle as her eyes lit up. Then she told a friend about it, and the snowball started to roll. The end of October I gave a talk on publishing and mentioned my idea and four more people were interested. It wasn't just an idea anymore, it was a reality. So I crafted an invitation letter, created a book cover, and assembled a web page with the details, and I sent my book idea out to the world. I only needed 20 women, 20 passionate women with inspiring stories, to collaborate with me. How hard could that be?

I contacted over 70 people and waited.

And waited.

And waited.

Four of the 70 people politely responded with a "no." I didn't hear from anyone else.

In the meantime, Doubt and Worry threw a party and invited their pals. Uncertainty came with Anxiety and Fear. Unworthiness flirted with Impatience and Inadequacy, and Confusion sat in a corner with Helplessness and Hopelessness. With all of their "assistance," it was easy to think the book wouldn't happen.

Then one person gave a resounding *yes*! Hope smiled. And I was overjoyed. It just takes time, I told myself. People are busy. Give them a chance.

Weeks passed. Hope curled into a little ball and my faith plummeted.

I saw Mindy again and we discussed my Soul Aspect, the energy body nearest to God or Spirit. Put one hand on your heart, she instructed, and reach out with your other hand to touch your Soul body. Then spread your wings. I imagined making contact with this body of light. I imagined my wings, rows and rows of grey and white feathers, lined up with precision, fluffy and soft and strong enough to last through the ages. As I pictured these wings my heart bloomed and swelled with so much love. Then she played a Deepak Chopra meditation tape about love. Your heart has the answers, Deepak said. I nodded mentally in agreement. Of course it does. That's F.A.I.T.H.

I listened to the meditation, drifted with the music, and pictured the *F.A.I.T.H.* book surrounded with love, blessed with love, and this gorgeous book of inspiring stories sprouted wings and flew out into the world. When I got home I created my F.A.I.T.H. vision statement, complete with wings, reaching #1 on Amazon, going viral like the *Chicken Soup for the Soul* books, touching people's hearts, helping them let go of old beliefs, and making a huge difference in the world. I started reading the statement every day, feeling the excitement build within me. I held the opening lines close to my heart: "Learning to trust. Being in the space of love instead of doubt. Knowing that the Universe would deliver in the right time. That's what F.A.I.T.H. is all about."

Helplessness and Hopelessness vanished into the ether.

Before Christmas I had six slots filled. More than a quarter of the collaborators I needed. The first milestone! But over Christmas and the week after I worried and doubted. *Where will I find the rest? I'm not going to find anyone. I might as well give up now.*

Goethe wrote, "At the moment of commitment the entire universe conspires to assist you." On New Year's Day I committed to the Universe that I'm doing this project. I drop-kicked Confusion and Inadequacy out the door and vowed that I would not quit.

Within the first week of the new year four more collaborators signed on. I'd reached the second milestone. Ten! One woman added a thoughtful note to her message and said, "I know finding partners has been slow for you, but the right people will show up." What a lift!

On January 6 I listened to a teleseminar with Marci Shimoff and Debra Poneman about a year-long coaching program called Your Year of Miracles. I wanted miracles. I needed miracles. And I wanted to learn how to create miracles. But a year-long program? Surely that would cost thousands of dollars that I couldn't afford. Marci's soothing voice lifted me and calmed me and spoke to that place inside that said "have no fear." So I put aside my worries and waited for the pitch. And when it came I laughed. Every month she and Debra would do a coaching call, a well-known spiritual/metaphysical celebrity would do a coaching call, and an energy healer would do a call, and all for $597. Not the thousands I had envisioned but a more than reasonable price.

The Universe was speaking loud and clear. I signed up on the spot. And on the first call with Marci and Debra, I decided on my theme for the year—*trust*—and pasted a "TRUST" sticky note on my computer. I knew without trust I would never get my project underway. But would I be able to trust and let go and be open?

The next few days crawled by. Impatience camped out in my living room and spun my thoughts into dread. What good are ten collaborators if no one else shows up? I can't do a book with only half of the people. What do I do now?

If every day I just sat and stared at my computer my thoughts would drive me crazy. Thankfully, gratefully, I had appointments. I spoke with a woman from a networking group about the book on Wednesday. I talked with a woman over lunch on Thursday. Saturday was a Feng Shui class and another opportunity to meet people. Anxiety spread her wings across my calendar and shadowed every move, yet somehow I eased her aside and moved on.

The following Tuesday I met an interested woman at a networking event. Almost a week later she became #11.

Mid-January came. Then another week passed. A coaching client contacted me about helping her to write her book. We had a wonderful conversation about spirituality and overcoming challenges. She signed up for a coaching session and my intuition told me she was perfect for the book. But I couldn't bring myself to ask. I was afraid of overwhelming her. She wouldn't want to take on something else, would she?

I wrestled with Unworthiness for three long days and finally pinned it with an inescapable hold. Then I called my new client. And from that discussion, she signed on (#12).

Thank you, Universe!

It was the end of January, three months from the start of the project. I now had enough slots filled for a decent sized book. I was thrilled. I notified the group with "Houston, we're a go!" and the collaborators responded with excitement.

TRUST ME!

Sometimes "trust" means letting go. Stepping back from the edge. Creating space. Wondering who would sign up next heightened my fear instead of calming it. Other areas of my life were expanding with little effort. I sold the first *F.A.I.T.H.* book (and it wasn't even written). I was invited to participate "for free" in a new Deepak Chopra online program about health and aging. If I could create those events, I could "allow" the book to happen. So I closed all my lists and reminders.

My Miracles Coaching program picked up again with the topic of self-love. Each day I was to focus on doing something fun. Fun was not wallowing in pity. Fun was making butterflies, laughing at silly TV comedy, dancing. We also talked about forgiveness. Forgive yourself when you make a mistake, when you feel you've said the wrong thing. I thought about past conversations with women where I'd spoken from desperation rather than love. I replayed the times I'd tried to argue or coerce. Then I took a walk and said the Ho'oponopono prayer: I'm sorry, please forgive me, thank you, I love you. I cradled Fear in my arms and crooned to her, over and over, and watched her turn into Calm.

Over the weekend I learned that I can give my angels a deadline. What's the point of "waiting" for something to happen when you can specify the time frame? I dialed up my angels and told them I wanted two more collaborators in 48 hours.

They responded. Disaster hit. One of my authors respectfully bowed out.

I fell into the abyss of no return. I wanted more, not less. So I sat down with my angels and impatiently asked for the perfect number of people for *F.A.I.T.H.* They said 12. I mentally nodded. I had 11 people; I could find one more. Not a problem. But I wanted to confirm the number. 12, right? Eight popped into my mind. I was confused. I asked again and saw 22, then 14. Exasperated, I demanded, "Are you telling me there is no perfect number?" The answer was a resounding *Yes. It doesn't matter. It's not how many people are in the book, it's about the energy. The right people are in the book.*

The thought took hold and spun through my mind. My body relaxed, my breath deepened, and I truly let go. And in that glorious stillness, Impatience grabbed Doubt and Worry and fled into the darkness.

I placed my hands over my heart and whispered, "Thank you." For the first time since the project began, I was at peace. Eleven people were just fine.

One week later another collaborator joined the project (#12). On March 3, another became lucky 13. And nine days later, the ranks swelled to 14.

Faith does not come easily to me. I'm envious of those people whose faith is rooted in unshakeable conviction. I want to know, without any doubt or worry, that I am connected. That I am one with everything. That I am truly a spiritual being having a human experience. Sometimes I feel those moments of bliss. Sometimes peace rocks me in its loving arms and I am safe. Sometimes joy flits in to my awareness like a graceful butterfly. But often my life is filled with difficult spaces where I have to make conscious choices.

Life presents constant challenges. How you respond determines the life you create. My path was littered with negative emotions—hopelessness, helplessness, confusion, inadequacy, impatience, unworthiness, anxiety, worry, and doubt. Emotions that used to leave me paralyzed. Healing the wounds of my past (the painful experiences and limiting beliefs) allowed me to build my confidence and finally to speak up. I gathered enough courage to breathe through the moment and take the next step. And through that trust I vanquished my fears.

It doesn't matter what method or program you use to clear those beliefs—prayer, talking to angels, energy healing, coaching, seminars and workshops, yoga, breathing. The list is endless. What's important is to find something that works for you.

This book came together with many leaps of faith. Because I overcame my negativity, people appeared and committed to the project, and their stories filled the pages. Doubt and Worry climbed on my shoulders numerous times and filled my mind with lies. But with the grace of Spirit, I pushed them aside and clung to my truth. It took effort. It took choice. It wasn't always easy. But *finding answers in the heart* is the best way I know to live my dream.

Are you ready to live your dream?

Nanette Littlestone, owner of Words of Passion, works with inspirational authors to overcome writers block, master correct grammar, create strong structure, and write with clarity and passion. She specializes in helping women write from the heart so they can put their passion into words and inspire others. www.wordsofpassion.com

There is a light which shines beyond the world, beyond everything, beyond the highest heaven. This is the light which shines within your heart.

– Upanishads

Epilogue

A re you ready to live your dream?

Your life is a miracle. Every moment, every breath, every step that you took along your path began from a place of love. As you learn to "be" in that place of love and compassion and forgiveness, you expand your presence in this world. You bring in more light. You make it possible for the world to heal.

It's time for everyone to experience this light. Miracles are present every moment. The more you create miracles for yourself, the easier it is for those around you to create them as well.

Be the spark that ignites your family and your community. Be aware of the miracles in your life. Let them grow and prosper. Let them stretch far and wide. Witness the sparkle of light around you and around everyone you see. You can make a difference. You can be who you're meant to be. All it takes is a little F.A.I.T.H.

About the Authors

Sheri Bagwell

Sheri Bagwell is a health and wellness coach. Her personalized healing plans combine nutritional guidance, energy work, and meditation. When you work with Sheri you learn to connect with your body, heal it, and take back your power for your health and your life.

The release of pain and the unfolding of your fully functioning heart, mind, and body is one of Sheri's true delights. She enjoys nothing more than reminding your body how to function and watching you move from pain and confusion to feeling freedom in your brain and body. She loves to watch your life flow more easily and know you are more connected to Source and are enjoying life.

As part of Dr. Jacob Teitelbaum's Practioners Alliance Network, Sheri is trained in all the systems of the body and understands how they are connected. Prescribing pharmaceutical quality supplements to support your body and your mind is key in regaining your health and wellness.

Sheri hosts amazing group classes and workshops like her signature flowing breath and energy meditation, and finding freedom from female problems. She also designs programs for people with excess body weight and chronic conditions like fibromyalgia and chronic fatigue. In addition, Sheri is available for weekend retreats in locations of your choice. Please contact her if you would like to host one of these classes or workshops or check out her website for the current class schedule.

Sheri's husband and son are God's greatest gifts to her.

770.235.7599
Sheri@sheribagwell.com
www.sheribagwell.com
Facebook – Sheri Bagwell The Pain Eraser

169

Tammy Billups

Tammy was a successful top biller for a nationwide recruiting firm in 1999 when her life dramatically shifted due to several unexpected losses near and dear to her heart. Intuitive gifts and childhood memories she had long repressed resurfaced, which set in motion a deep inner healing journey and new path in life via a gentle healing method called Bioenergetics. She saw remarkable results with her body, emotions, and behavior. Chronic physical ailments virtually disappeared. Daily medications were no longer needed as she embraced an overall healthier lifestyle.

Tammy's mastery of Bioenergy Healing was propelled forward by her natural gifts for experiencing energy and her personal healing journey. She began working with individuals and animals in 2001, utilizing her highly intuitive healing gifts that were honed through training at The Center for Integrative Therapy.

Her group seminars and workshops over the last decade focus on deepening self-love and nurturing, and getting connected through various methods like meditation, dream interpretation, essential oils, and techniques to gently release stress and anxiety. One of her passions is sharing her discoveries about the spiritual relationship between animals and their people. She's currently working on her book *Beyond the Fur*, a guide to help people understand and interpret their animal companions' ingenious messages. With that awareness both the individuals and their animals can grow, heal, and love more deeply.

Tammy is a Certified Bioenergetics Interface Therapist, Certified Healer for Animals, an Ordained Inter-Faith Minister, and is trained in Healing Touch for Animals®.

tammy@sundancehealing.com
www.tammybillups.com
Twitter – sundancehealing
Facebook – www.facebook.com/sundancehealing

Paula Flint

Paula Flint is a Life Coach who helps men and women who are facing difficult challenges in their lives—physically, mentally, emotionally, and spiritually. A grandmother now, Paula opened her office in 2011 to help people understand and accept that life sometimes offers them challenges that initially feel insurmountable. She teaches that patience and a little help from someone who has been there and is not afraid to share her own experiences allow her clients not only to overcome the challenges but to triumph.

Prior to opening her office at the Heal Your Life Center in Bridgeport, West Virginia, Paula graduated with a Master's in Counseling Psychology and became a member of the ECK Clergy. Today Paula offers a wide range of programs and services from individual and group sessions to seminars.

She states, "Life Coaching is very different from therapy or counseling. It is a collaboration between two people to facilitate personal growth. My clients and I work together to uncover the grandest version of who they perceive themselves to be. I am not here to change anyone; I am here to help others open up to who they already are."

Paula is currently working on her book *Life Coach: Coached by Life*. She deeply dissects her own triumphs and defeats and her life-long search for spiritual awareness. She describes how, from before birth, life has been her personal coach, a conscious companion.

304.842.6160
LifeCoach@hotmail.com
www.Lifecoach147.com
Facebook – Paula Flint (Bridgeport, WV)
LinkedIn – Paula Flint, MA

Julie Flippin

Julie Flippin, owner of Small Business Savvy, is a business coach who works with courageous, passionate small business owners who are committed to being more profitable. For 30+ years Julie worked as a controller, sales manager, and HR Specialist. But it wasn't until she opened her own Accounting/ Bookkeeping business that she started to understand what it took to be in business "for yourself."

To understand more about human behavior, she went back to school and created a thriving counseling practice. Through her expertise, she helped her clients move through fear, worry, and procrastination and become the best they could be.

Ten years later she turned her career to business coaching and founded Small Business Savvy with a focus on profitability. Julie takes the fear out of marketing and sales and creates strong, workable strategies for business entrepreneurs to achieve their goals. It is her privilege to teach and encourage her clients on their journeys and support them in the ultimate result—creating success.

julie@smallbusinesssavvy.com
www.SmallBusinessSavvy.com
Twitter – JulieFlippin
Facebook – Small Business Savvy

Betty Humphrey Fowler

Betty Humphrey Fowler is a Feng Shui Consultant, Certified Interior Re-designer, author, speaker, and workshop presenter. The passion she has for her business, Energized Spaces, stems from her belief that everyone deserves to live and work in happy, healthy, thriving spaces. She is a lifelong student and enjoys sharing what she learns with others. Her goal is to help Feng Shui become a mainstream topic in our society.

Betty received her Bachelor of Science degree in Physical Education and served as the head fitness instructor at The Public Safety Training Center in Santa Rosa, California for 17 years. There she taught lifetime and job-related fitness and stress management skills to over 3,000 police and fire academy recruits. To handle the stress of working varied hours, being married to a police officer, and raising two young children, she was guided to study Feng Shui. The information she learned helped her create peace and organization in her physical environment, which created peace and calm in her and her family's life.

Betty helps clients going through life-changing events shift the energy in their living spaces to move forward and renew their enthusiasm for life. She currently lives in the metro Atlanta area and offers private consultations, group presentations, and workshops.

betty@energizedspaces.com
www.energizedspaces.com

Colleen Humphries

Colleen Humphries is an RN, Reiki Master, author, and certified Law of Attraction Life Coach for nurses and other professional women who are suffering from the burnout that affects their lives mentally, emotionally, physically, and spiritually. After working with Colleen, these women feel alive again, are able to take back control of their lives (personally and professionally), return to balance, and regain what is really important to them—time for themselves and their families.

Through teaching Jack Canfield's Success Principles, Colleen helps her clients to go from where they are to where they want to be further, faster, and with less effort. She has recently started working with women who are experiencing the money-burnout-blues, guiding them to experience abundance in all aspects of their lives.

One of her passions is putting on seminars on Burnout Relief and Principles of Success that are very experiential to lock in the learning to show the participants how powerful they really are.

Colleen is the author of the free eBook *The ABCs of Deliberately Creating Your Life* and the free article called *Your Rx for Relief from Burnout,* which are available on her website. She is currently working on the book *No Longer Creating by Default, The ABCs of Deliberately Creating Your Life.* You can also hear Colleen on her radio show *Think About It,* an all-holistic, alternative, outside-the-box, and universal-law based program to give the listeners something to "think about" to move them forward in their lives.

410.670.3289
colleen@colleenhumphries.com
www.ColleenHumphries.com
Twitter – ColleenRNCoach
Facebook – Colleen A Kahler Humphries / Colleen's Radio Show
LinkedIn – Colleen (Kahler) Humphries

ABOUT THE AUTHORS

Nanette
Littlestone

Nanette Littlestone loves playing with words, Roget's Thesaurus, and word puzzles. Writing that flows is thrilling. Writer's block is not. She's also intuitive, heart-centered, slightly irreverent, and has a wacky sense of humor which she offsets with a generous smile.

Nanette is a writing coach, editor, author, and CEO of Words of Passion. She helps inspirational authors overcome writers block, master correct grammar, create strong structure, and write with clarity and passion by blending the technicalities of writing with intuition, emotion, and heart. Twenty years of experience working with both fiction and nonfiction (plus advanced degrees in Resistance, Doubt, and Worry) kindle Nanette's passion for assisting authors to achieve their own unique message. She specializes in helping women write from the heart so they can put their passion into words and inspire others. Finding that place of struggle within her clients and unlocking the door to create change and opportunity is what makes her heart soar.

On the publishing side, Nanette believes that becoming an author doesn't have to be difficult. She created the Partner Up! Book Program to help women entrepreneurs get published the easy way through collaborative books. She is also the editor and coauthor of two *Easy Weekly Meals* electronic cookbooks, editor and coauthor of *The 28-Day Thought Diet*, and author of the forthcoming book *Overcoming Writer's Block: Moving from Fear to Passion*. Her coaching programs and services offer clients unique and in-depth ways to strengthen their manuscripts and make their writing sing.

nanette@wordsofpassion.com
www.wordsofpassion.com
Facebook – Nanette Littlestone/Words of Passion
LinkedIn – Nanette Littlestone

Ricia L. Maxie

An internationally renowned intuitive consultant/mystic, Reiki practitioner, and speaker, Ricia loves to help people with her God-given ability. She uses prayer and meditation to deepen her readings and connect with spirit guides, angels, and those who have passed beyond this physical dimension.

Born with intuitive gifts that continued to expand through the years, Ricia received training from a variety of teachers and guides in body and not in body. She uses a range of skills, combined with her gifts, which include clairvoyance, clairaudience, claircognizance, clairsentience, mediumship, and channeling.

For thirty years, Ricia has been helping people find the answers they need. Services include intuitive consultations, spiritual and intuitive development classes, workshops, retreats, guided meditation, past life regressions, hypnosis, Reiki, and personal growth coaching.

Ricia L. Maxie is also a change management and organization development consultant who is an experienced facilitator, coach, and instructor. She teaches communication and collaboration at all levels of an organization and facilitates team building, interest-based problem solving, and conflict resolution. She has coached executives and employees on leadership techniques and effective communication, which results in increased morale. Processes for organization-wide change initiatives or simply department level accord have been her specialty.

Ricia earned a BA in psychology from Dominican University and an MA in counseling psychology from the University of San Francisco.

707.280.2404 (Can receive calls or text)
ricialm@aol.com
www.RiciaLMaxie.com
Facebook – Ricia L. Maxie Intuitive

Michelle Mechem

Michelle Mechem is a Residential Realtor in Atlanta, GA. Prior to Real Estate she spent ten years in Accounting Management between Arthur Andersen and VIACOM. In 1999 she was voted WUPA-TV Atlanta's employee of the year.

After helping others run their businesses she decided to start her own and began a career in real estate in spring of 2002. She joined Keller Williams Intown Atlanta in November 2002 and joined forces with Hunter as a partner in the Hunter Group in May of 2003. In their first full year together, they were the 6th highest producing team in the Southeast Region. She specializes in Atlanta's Intown neighborhoods and the close-in suburbs. She believes *home* is the starting place for a fabulous life and works hard for her clients to both buy and sell their biggest investment.

Michelle has always had a passion for writing and was the Real Estate Columnist for *The Sunday Paper*, a weekly newspaper, from 2005–2008. She also began the blog www.ThrivingInRealEstate.com to assist other agents with their business. She began officially coaching in April 2009.

She is married to Robert Mechem, car whisperer and restoration wizard extraordinaire. They ride motorcycles, travel, and squeeze every drop of joy possible out of life. They live in a historic school circa 1900, in the Kirkwood neighborhood of Atlanta, with their mountain lion-sized cats Rocky and Ding.

404.631.6266
Michelle@HouseHunterAtlanta.com
www.HouseHunterAtlanta.com

Linda Minnick

Linda Minnick is a certified life coach, Professional PSYCH-K® Facilitator, Certified Doreen Virtue Angel Card Reader, and a specialist in transformational thinking. She has shared the stage with world-renowned teachers such as Mary Morrissey, Bob Proctor, and Michael Beckwith. She has studied the works of Dr. Wayne Dyer, Dr. Bruce Lipton, and many other internationally recognized transformational thinking specialists.

As a sought-after coach, speaker, and trainer, Linda has offered transformational coaching and workshops to individuals and organizations around the country. Whether it's individual coaching or group presentations, Linda helps her clients ignite the potential within them to attain the results they have been looking for, and she gives them the tools to continue on that upward spiral of fulfillment and success.

Born and raised in South St. Louis, Linda currently lives outside of Atlanta in Roswell, Georgia with her husband John. They have been married 39 years and have four adult children and two grandchildren.

lkminnick@live.com
www.lindaminnick.com

Laina Orlando

Laina Orlando, an Atlanta resident for the past 27 years, is a writer, speaker, Awareness Coach, and author of The Power of Awareness Program. She is the founder of The Center for Awareness which is committed to serving as a resource of educational and experiential processes that guide seekers on the Journey that leads to Spiritual Awakening. Since 2007, Laina has been an active member within Atlanta's spiritual community, speaking, teaching, or leading workshops in various centers, including Unity Churches, The Spiritual Living Center, and various corporate organizations such as Kennestone Hospital.

An ordinary woman, who has undergone an extraordinary spiritual transformation, Laina takes a fresh and fun approach to simplifying spirituality for today's seekers of truth. Laina's own awakening inspires her to share what is possible when one truly commits to navigating the path of self-awareness. By investigating our personal psychology and general worldviews, we become aware of the limiting beliefs we have been conditioned to accept about ourselves and others, which cause us to have a fear-based and limited experience of life. Through simple techniques, humor, and timeless wisdom, Laina transforms weighty spiritual concepts into practical bite-sized morsels that can be easily applied to everyday life. Laina's mantra: Life is fun and easy. Her mission: to awaken humanity to the magnificence within.

Laina@ThePowerofAwareness.com
www.lainaorlando.com
Twitter – LainaOrlando
Facebook – Laina Orlando, Awareness Coach

Bonnie Salamon

Bonnie Salamon knows what it is to overcome severe self-doubt and crippling agoraphobia to become a well-known and celebrated speaker, facilitator, and coach for those seeking meaning and purpose in the later years of life.

In the "dark ages" of mental health issues (the 1960s through 1980s), hardly anyone acknowledged the problems surrounding subjects like depression and agoraphobia. For Bonnie, her teen and young adult years were marred by the fear that, at any moment, these maladies would again overtake her, causing her to "drop out" of school, jobs, and anything else that made up a normal life. Historically, that had been the case.

With the love and patience of family, friends, and mentors, and the faith that she was meant for more than her stifling stay-at-home life, she eventually followed a string of Spirit-driven opportunities to learn, participate, and expand, and to go back to college after 39 years and finish the degree that agoraphobia prevented. She began her mid-life journey and studied to become a facilitator of spiritual connection programs, a coach to support mid-lifers as they reached for meaning in the later stages of life, and the creator of "Nourished Soul: Caring for Your Youniverse," a live multi-day, multi-speaker event held in the Atlanta area.

Bonnie lives on beautiful Lake Lanier, Georgia with her beloved husband of 45 years. They share a loving relationship with their son, daughter-in-law, and granddaughter. Bonnie lives each day in gratitude for the chances she has been given to fulfill her life purpose.

404.502.0497
bsalamon@autumnsfire.org
www.autumnsfire.org
Facebook – Bonnie Salamon
LinkedIn – Bonnie Salamon

ABOUT THE AUTHORS

Randi Shapiro

Randi Shapiro is the President of Recruiting Specialists, Inc., a national boutique recruitment and staffing firm based in Atlanta, Georgia. Randi founded the company in 2002 and possesses over two decades worth of recruiting industry experience. She prides herself on delivering top talent to small, medium, and Fortune 500 companies in Marketing, Advertising, HR, Office Management, and Executive Support, as well as Executive search. Prior to founding Recruiting Specialists, Randi spent 15 years as an accomplished recruiter and business development professional with her late mother's successful and greatly respected search firm in Atlanta.

Randi is not only an entrepreneur and recruiter, she is also a tenacious and determined relationship builder and motivator, a coach for her candidates, valued counsel to her clients, and everyone's unabashed "cheerleader." Her clients and candidates describe Randi as a passionate pro who truly enjoys and thrives on the relationships she has developed over the years with all of the talented people she has encountered.

While Randi lives and breathes to work and provide service to others, she also enjoys a strong cup of coffee, old movies, shopping, sunshine, and spending time in the kitchen. She has been married for 28 years to the love of her life, longtime Atlanta sports radio talk show host Mitch Evans of 92.9 *The Game*. They live in Woodstock, Georgia with their favorite four-legged friend, Lillie the Cat.

randi@recruitingspec.com
www.recruitingspec.com
LinkedIn – Randi Shapiro

Mindy Strich

Mindy Strich found her way to energy medicine after a successful career in operations and management. After 25 years of seeking traditional medical solutions for a lifelong battle with an unknown chronic illness, she enrolled at The Whitewinds Institute of Energetic Healing to resolve the health issues that had afflicted her most of her life. Studying with Dr. Fernand Poulin, one of the leading voices in energy medicine, her training enabled her to explain her illness, transform her health, and heal from the unexpected end of her marriage. Today Mindy is a certified Reiki, Healing Touch International, and I.E.M. (Integrative Energy Medicine) Energetic Healing Practitioner. The owner of Healing Hearts, LLC, Mindy is now assisting clients on their own paths to healing. Mindy is also an Ordained Minister and a shamanic Pachakuti Mesa Carrier.

Mindy continues her work with Dr. Poulin as teaching assistant to first year students at Whitewinds and is the facilitator of "Heartache to Healing," a monthly support group directed at women who are facing separation and divorce. She is a co-author of *The 28-Day Thought Diet*, written to encourage readers to choose thoughts that support and empower their lives, and the co-promoter of "Good Karma," a social networking group for spiritually inspired women in the Atlanta area.

For more information on energy healing or to contact Mindy, visit her website at www.healingheartenergy.com.

Twitter – MindyStrich
Facebook – Healing Hearts LLC
Meetup – Heartbreak to Healing – Renewing Your Life After Divorce

Volume 2

Do you have a personal story of triumph to share? If you're like the women in this book who have overcome challenges in their lives through perseverance, determination, and faith, then we invite you to participate in the Second Volume of *F.A.I.T.H.* Millions of people around the world deserve to be healthier, stronger, more courageous, following their passions. Help us to help them by sharing inspiration.

Please visit www.FindingAnswersInTheHeart.com/participation for more information.

Thank you for reading *F.A.I.T.H.*

We encourage you to connect with the authors
using the contact information listed on their bios.

If you'd like more F.A.I.T.H.,
please sign up for the newsletter at
www.FindingAnswersInTheHeart.com

Share your comments about F.A.I.T.H.
by emailing comments@FindingAnswersInTheHeart.com